W9-BDR-719

DISCARD

STORIES OF A WORKFORCE

CELEBRATING THE CENTENNIAL OF THE HOUSTON SHIP CHANNEL

[**EXHIBITION**] Pat Jasper, Angel Quesada and Danielle Burns

[**CATALOG**] Pat Jasper and Carl Lindahl with contributions from
Danielle Burns, Rati Ramadas Girish, Christina Grubitz, Gabriella Flournoy and Linda Ho Peche

[**RESEARCH AND EDITORIAL ASSISTANCE**] Harold Dodd, Gabriella Flournoy, Rati Ramadas Girish, Christina Grubitz,
Carl Lindahl, Rebecca Marvil, Linda Ho Peche, Betsy Peterson, Anthony Potozniack and David Theis

PRESENTING SPONSOR

ADDITIONAL SUPPORT

Susan Vaughan Foundation Inc

HOUSTON ENDOWMENT INC.
A PHILANTHROPY ENDOWED BY MR. AND MRS. JESSE H. JONES

ART WORKS.
arts.gov

ISBN 978-0-692-27476-7
Library of Congress Cataloging-in-Publication Data on file with Houston Arts Alliance
Design: Cregan Design

[TABLE OF CONTENTS]

[**TO**]

Gina, for figuring me out and loving me all the more;

Harold, for giving me more support than anyone deserves;

Carl, for his stellar intellectual and ethical guidance;

Angel, for commitment above and beyond the call;

*All people who accepted that I was an outsider
but still agreed talked to me about the Port.*

— **PAT JASPER**

THE PORT OF HOUSTON: *A Brief Historical Overview*

On August 30, 1836, the city of Houston was established when two entrepreneurial brothers from New York, Augustus Chapman Allen and John Kirby Allen, ran an advertisement in the *Telegraph and Texas Register* for the "Town of Houston." The town, which featured a mixture of timber and grassland, lay on the level coastal plain. The brothers claimed that the town would become "the great interior commercial emporium of Texas," that ships from New York and New Orleans could sail up Buffalo Bayou to its door. Now one of the busiest waterways in the United States, the Houston Ship Channel has truly achieved its early promise to become the preeminent link between Texas and the sea.

Recognizing the potential of Buffalo Bayou, the Allen brothers laid out the town of Houston at the head of its navigable course. Many doubted that Buffalo Bayou, with a depth of only six feet at the time, was a possible waterway. To demonstrate that steamships could navigate the stream, the entrepreneurs hired the eighty-five-foot *Laura*, the smallest steamer they could find, to travel the five and one-and-a-half miles from the town of Harrisburg to Houston. The journey took three days. With the success of this first trial, a movement that would span decades and ultimately produce a deep-water port began. In 1841, the city passed an ordinance officially recognizing the Port of Houston and boats began using the bayou on a regular schedule.

From the 1850s through the early 1900s, the waterway was improved and organizations and improvements on the Port were established. The Houston Navigation Company, later the Houston Direct Navigation Company, an organization of Houston merchants and steamboats, dominated navigation on the bayou. Businesses were booming and steamboats operated regularly between Houston and Galveston carrying both passengers and cargo. Cotton was the primary item transported on these ships.

With frequent use of the waterway, Houston leaders began to discuss ways in which it could be improved to ensure the flourishing of commerce. Port authorities laid plans to enlarge the bayou. The planners received added support in 1870 when Houston was designated as a port of entry by the United States government. Over the next two decades, Houston became the rail crossroads of Texas and Port traffic increased as goods were transferred from railcars to ship on their journey to distant points.

The Port had been dredged to accommodate more types of ships; however, the lack of deep water concerned Houston businessmen. During the 1890s, U.S. Representative Tom Ball began to lobby his congressional colleagues to support a deep-water port for Houston. This general effort coincided with a devastating hurricane and flood in Galveston in September 1900, creating one of the worst disasters in American history. More than eight thousand lost their lives and much of the island city and its commercial infrastructure were swept away.

Tom Ball proposed an innovative concept. He suggested that Houston share the cost with the federal government for dredging a deep-water channel to Houston. Congressional committee members were amazed by the bold proposal from Houston and the representatives voted unanimously to accept the "Houston Plan."

The Harris County Houston Ship Channel Navigation District was formed, and a campaign was launched to persuade voters to approve $1.25 million in bonds to pay for the District's share of the waterway. The voters carried the measure by a majority of sixteen to one. However, the bonds needed to be sold. Legendary Houston millionaire businessman Jesse H. Jones would be a major force in the Port's destiny. He personally asked each Houston bank to accept the bonds. In just twenty-four hours, he persuaded all the banks to buy shares. It was an investment that has paid off many times over.

Work on the deep channel commenced in 1912. Similar precedent-setting maritime projects of the time were the Gulf Intracoastal Waterway and the fifty-one-mile long Panama Canal. On the morning of September 7, 1914, the dredge boat Texas signaled by whistles the completion of work on the Channel. An official ceremony to celebrate its opening was held Tuesday morning, November 10, 1914. Thousands of people attended. From his office in Washington, D.C., President Woodrow Wilson fired a cannon via remote control to officially mark the Channel as ready for world commerce.

By 1919, ships departed from the Port of Houston for ports on the eastern seaboard, but also for those across the Atlantic Ocean. The *S.S. Merrymount* transported the first direct shipment of cotton to Liverpool, England, and within a decade Houston would become the United States' leading cotton port. As demand for oil exploded in the early twentieth century, petroleum soon rivaled cotton as the most important cargo. The booming oil trade fostered yet another campaign to increase the depth of the Ship Channel. As Houston became an important center of the petroleum industry, it needed to accommodate the increased number of oil tankers navigating its length.

Despite a brief interruption during the Great Depression, by 1930 nine refineries were operating along the Channel, elevating the Port of Houston to third in the nation in terms of total tonnage. In 1937, the Port reached the status of second only to New York in tonnage and importance, according to *Fortune* magazine.

Brought to prominence during World War II was the demand for petroleum products. It inspired the development of synthetic rubber as a byproduct of petroleum to compensate for the interruption of trade in natural rubber. Two synthetic rubber plants were built near the Channel, the beginnings of the petrochemical industrial complex for which Houston has become known. The postwar years also saw the Port become a major hub for grain shipments from the Midwest—lifting total tonnage to second in the nation by 1948.

The first major change in sea transportation came to the Port of Houston in 1956 with the era of containerized shipping. A shipment of fifty-eight loaded containers, transported on the *Ideal X* from New York to Houston, was part of a history-making expedition. Containerized shipping revolutionized cargo transportation by making it possible to ship tons of goods as a single unit. Port officials realized that the local ports were now competing not only with the country but with worldwide ports and facilities. To compete, once again, the waterways had to be enlarged.

Developed by the Port of Houston Authority, the Houston World Trade Building was the first facility of its kind in the country. The $3.5-million dollar structure, designed as a central location for international trade interests, opened January 29, 1962, and the building housed consular offices, transportation companies, importers and exporters. In 1977, the Port opened the Barbours Cut Terminal, the first dedicated container port in Texas, and now one of the premier container-handling facilities on the U.S. Gulf Coast. The Port continues to pioneer new technologies, introducing the double-stack train in 1981. The placement of one container on top of another reduced transportation costs substantially.

Environmental protection became a priority around the turn of the twenty-first century. In 2000, the Environmental Protection Agency (EPA) selected the Port of Houston as the only port to be trained in the creation of sophisticated environmental management systems. This was the beginning of a long string of firsts for the Port of Houston Authority (PHA). The PHA became the first U.S. port authority to conduct air emissions testing on off-road equipment, the first U.S. port authority with an environmental management meeting the internationally recognized standards for environmental excellence (2002), and the first to be recertified under the new standards for its environmental management system.

Today, the Port of Houston is the main port in the state of Texas and the world's tenth largest port. The growth of the Port of Houston during its first century has been incomparable, and the Houston Ship Channel is a testimony to the hard work, diligence and perseverance of its founding fathers. It continues to link Houston to the world and the world to our great city. ▮

Ship Portrait, *Fortune Epoch at City Docks*
Photo by Lou Vest

STORIES OF A WORKFORCE:
Celebrating the Centennial of the Houston Ship Channel

THE PORT OF HOUSTON IS THE GREAT HIDDEN ENGINE of the city's prosperity. More than one-quarter of the metropolitan area's 2.6 million jobs belong to people who work the Port and its related industries, and everyone in the region is affected at least indirectly by the wealth that has flowed from around the world into the mouth of Buffalo Bayou. The Port itself is a massive geographic complex: a constellation of docks, warehouses, railheads, refineries and heavy machinery stretching some fifty miles along the Ship Channel that connects Houston to the Gulf of Mexico. These structures exist for the sake of the water traffic: numberless vessels, at dock or in motion, ranging from tiny pilot boats, to sturdy tugs, to the massive cargo ships, more than one thousand feet in length, that vie in size with many of the buildings that line the Channel.

It is hard to imagine an economic landmark of such size and importance, and yet so well concealed, as the Port of Houston. The massive Port of New York, in contrast, is plainly visible in almost any panoramic view of Manhattan; its docks may be seen from the Henry Hudson Freeway or any of the city's tallest buildings; one of the nation's most visited tourist attractions, the Statue of Liberty, offers a commanding view of the port's traffic. The Port of Houston sees far more cargo than the Port of New York, yet a Houston resident can drive the entire web of the city's major roads and highways and find only a few wisps of evidence that the Port exists. If you look down from the quarter-mile stretch of Interstate 610 East that rises far into the air to span the Ship Channel, you may see one of the massive cargo ships in motion; driving Beltway 8 East, two miles south of Interstate 10, will take you over another stretch of the Channel. Most Houstonians have to drive far out of their normal commuter routes to reach these impressive but still very partial hints of the Port of Houston.

Already concealed by the geographic accidents of Houston's expansion, the Port was further concealed, strategically, in the wake of 9/11, as the Department of Homeland Security required Houston, like other American cities, to deter potential terrorist acts by rendering many previously accessible parts of the Port closed to the public. Workers who once brought family members down to the docks and warehouses to witness their work can no longer do so with ease. Job seekers hoping to secure employment for a day or a lifetime have a far more complicated task ahead of them than was the case fifteen years ago.

And when discussions of the Port and the Ship Channel have burst into public discourse, they almost invariably veer toward portraits of major institutions or corporate histories. Much information can be found on the Port of Houston Authority, or its Commissioners, or the major petrochemical corporations that reside there. These are generally the most frequent focus of attention and discussion. The exhibition, *Stories of a Workforce: Celebrating the Centennial of the Houston Ship Channel*, on the other hand, navigates away from that emphasis and considers instead the people involved: the men and women who make this complex economic entity operate through their work and participation in the many occupations that support the Port.

To share this previously unheard story we present the fruits of a project at least four years in the making. We began with a research effort funded by the American Folklife Center at the Library of Congress and entitled *Working the Port*, which allowed us to record more than fifty interviews from individuals working in a variety of occupations important to the commerce of the Port. As proud as we are of the project's goals and our efforts to range widely in gathering the stories of the very large and diverse community of Port workers, we know it is but a sampling. Nevertheless, we have sought to collect from a broad representation of professions, communities and genders. *Working the Port* has conducted, logged and archived interviews from the very individuals who make up the backbone of the city's economic engine. By documenting the stories from individuals who work the loading docks, or convene in board rooms, or crew the boats and ships, or ply shoreside trades, we have unlocked a new and important way to examine the city's history and its contemporary occupational, commercial and cultural life.

When it began, the *Working the Port* project was a simple but important exercise, an effort to make the Port of Houston better seen, better known and especially, better heard. By privileging the voices of the men and women who work there, *Working the Port* called on the greatest ground-level experts to tell us their stories, to share their experience, to relay information about an occupational setting that has been, like many other American workplaces, drastically transformed over the last several decades. In the process of undertaking the *Working the Port* interviews and listening to them over time, it became clear that certain themes were consistently articulated by many of the participants. These themes emerged naturally in the course of the interviews, driven by the participants' own perspectives on their experience. Most common of all, hands down, was a very real expression of pride in and respect for the work they and their fellow workers performed and accomplished on behalf of the region as a whole.

The unique and overarching trait of the exhibition, *Stories of a Workforce: Celebrating the Centennial of the Houston Ship Channel*, is the use of personal narratives; we highlight the stories that emerged from our initial interviews. In other words, the exhibition organization has largely been determined by the content of the interviews: the experiences, memories and concerns that the participants expressed through their stories. Thus, the vantage point of the exhibition, taking on the perspectives of the interviewees, is life and work on the Port over the last fifty or so years. We interviewed young people who could share what it was like entering today's workforce. We interviewed retirees, who could take us back further in their stories than most who are currently on the job, thus providing historical context and illuminating events that are many decades old. We interviewed individuals in the thick of their careers who could speak to the changes and outcomes that have played a central role in the work that they presently do. We are profoundly grateful for the candor and the honesty of all the people who shared their stories. Therefore, the exhibition, while it acknowledges the Port's history, is really a contemporary grassroots examination—through the words of the workers themselves—of the Houston Ship Channel and the Port of Houston. In a sense, it is a collective autobiography of the Ship Channel workers that this project has had the honor to document. It attempts to capture the living memory of the Port workforce.

Stories of a Workforce: Celebrating the Centennial of the Houston Ship Channel identifies and extracts salient themes that have consistently emerged from these memories as a means of organizing the exhibition and, by extension, the catalog. We have no doubt we have missed important issues, but we also believe we have captured views and information that are not well documented elsewhere. After a brief overview of the Ship Channel's history, the exhibition will address the recurrent themes that significantly inform the experiences of the Port workforce. They are represented in the catalog through the five following essays:

[**COMMUNITIES**] examines stories about the development of diverse and distinctive Houston-area neighborhoods and communities like the Mexican American-founded Magnolia Park and the African American neighborhood of Clinton Park that were formed by early Ship Channel workers.

[**GENERATIONS**] considers the importance of family tradition in the trades and professions that are practiced there and particularly tradition's role in fueling the workforce and elevating opportunities for Houston-area families over the years.

[**KNOW-HOW**] contemplates the nature of "knowledge" in the workplace and the relationship of local expertise learned on the job, in the environment and from each other, compared to the acquisition of contemporary, textbook-driven skills and abilities.

[**STRUGGLES**] broaches the question of the Port's unique and often surprising labor and management history, as well as the process of overcoming discriminatory practices, as understood through the lens and expressed in voices of individuals on all sides of these questions.

[**TRANSFORMATIONS**] traces the dramatic changes that have taken place in all of the above domains, as experienced and remembered by workers who discuss the evolution of the work, the workplace and the workforce on the Ship Channel.

In drawing upon these topics to structure the exhibition and the catalog , we are not making judgments about the last fifty years on the Port of Houston or the Houston Ship Channel. Instead, as we said earlier, we are trying to give voice and visibility and, in so doing, take seriously the character of work on the Ship Channel and how it has changed—using the workers' stories to heighten this awareness. As second-generation Houston Pilot Matthew Glass remarked:

> *It amazes me. When I lived in Downtown, I would tell people in the building I lived in, you know, they would ask me what I did. This was a year ago or so. I would tell people, "Oh I'm a harbor pilot." They'd say, "Oh, well what airline do you fly for?" I'd say, "No, I don't fly for an airline." They'd say, "Oh okay, so what airline do you work for?" It's amazing about how people don't know about the Port, but this is such a big city. It's unreal.*

But at the same time, we are eager to ensure, where opportunity provides, that this heightened visibility also leads to sharing interviewee stories that relay experiences that have significantly shaped, and even reshaped, the workforce. Thus, some of these narratives will, perforce, address events, recount incidents and describe occurrences that are difficult and problematic, frequently reflecting social practices and attitudes that are sometimes painful to acknowledge and digest. We include these because they construct a fuller picture of the workforce. We include these because they should rightly be a part of the public record. Most importantly, we include these because these are the experiences, memories and words of the Port workers.

For this same reason, we have included selected excerpts from twenty different interviews that further expand our understanding of the Houston Ship Channel and its diverse workforce. Many of these excerpts reiterate aspects of the issues addressed in the exhibition themes; but the text of many extends beyond these topics to illuminate more fully the world of work at the Port of Houston. A surprising aspect of these accumulated narratives, expressed time and again, is the organic way the many different sectors of the Ship Channel workforce have found or shaped a sense of common cause, even when it didn't fully benefit one sector or another. Understanding that a healthy, efficient and collaborative workforce created a productive and profitable work-place for all underlines many of the interviews. As Patrick Seeba of the Greater Houston Port Bureau points out:

The one thing I would say about Houston is we have a competitively cooperative culture that astounds people. When I go to meetings about a problem, you will see in the same room the ILA, the non-union steve-dores (who, in Houston, play in the community—whereas in other ports, maybe have a little more, not necessarily antagonistic, but nonexistent relationship with the community). You will see the ports, the private terminals and the competitors in the room…

I get drop-jawed from people who say, "How do you get them all in the same room?" I say, "You call them and you look at their schedule…"

"No, no, no, how do you get them to agree without their lawyers?" Lawyers are expensive, and by bringing them into the room, it makes it more expensive. I have nothing against them—they are critical in a lot of ways—but at the same time if you can talk to the guy who you actually have the issue with, you can solve it a lot faster. ∎

LOU
VEST

To CAPTURE *that* MOMENT

LOU VEST IS KNOWN AS "ONE-EIGHTEEN" BY HIS FELLOW PILOTS. AS THE 118TH MEMBER OF THE HOUSTON PILOTS ASSOCIATION, HE WORKS AMONG THE VERY FEW TO BE ENTRUSTED WITH ONE OF THE MOST DIFFICULT AND HONORED JOBS ON THE PORT: PILOTING GIANT CARGO SHIPS UP AND DOWN A FIFTY-MILE-LONG SLIVER OF WATER KNOWN AS THE HOUSTON SHIP CHANNEL. A LONG-TIME HOUSTON PILOT AS WELL AS AN ARTFUL PHOTOGRAPHER, LOU'S RARE ACCESS ALLOWS HIM TO CAPTURE IMAGES AND VIEW GALVESTON BAY AND THE SHIP CHANNEL FROM THE COMMANDING HEIGHTS OF A SHIP'S BRIDGE, AND TO FOCUS ON THE MEN AND WOMEN WHO WORK THE SHIPS AND DOCKS. HE SEES THE PORT AS THE LIVING PRODUCT OF A RELATIONSHIP AMONG TERMINAL OPERATORS, TUGBOATS, STEVEDORES, AGENTS, PILOTS AND A HOST OF OTHER WORKS AND ORGANIZATIONS, ALL PERFORMING THEIR SPECIALIZED TASKS IN AN ORGANIC WAY. HIS IMAGES OF THE PORT OF HOUSTON ARE A SINGULAR BLEND OF TALENT, EXPERIENCE, AND ACCESS. HIS PHOTOGRAPHS CAPTURE BOTH THE SURFACE BEAUTY AND INNER WORKINGS OF WHAT HE SEES, FOR HE IS BOTH A VISUAL ARTIST AND AN INSIDER WHO HAS PILOTED THE PORT'S WATERS FOR MORE THAN A QUARTER OF A CENTURY.

SINCE ABOUT 2000, LOU HAS BEEN PHOTOGRAPHING THE PORT OF HOUSTON. HE RECALLS ONE OF THE INCIDENTS THAT SPURRED HIM TO TAKE HIS CAMERA ON BOARD WITH HIM.

I had a job where I finished up about three in the morning, and I had to walk about a mile to get to my car down in the docks. And it was three in the morning. It was absolutely calm. There was a light rain falling. And the reflections of light in the water, the raindrops hitting the water, with the concentric splashes. And I'm walking down there, and there's all these ships, just ship after ship, and they're registered in Bombay and Bahamas and Cypress and Vanuatu, and they all have exotic names of one kind or another. And I thought, "Wow, you know, I could write a poem about this. I could use the exotic names of the ships." I even thought about writing down the names of the ships that day, but then I thought, "Ah, you could pick any day." It was really kind of a moving experience. There I am with the romance of going to sea: it was like Conrad, Kipling, you know, and I really enjoyed the moment. And that was before I started taking photos. I had been a photographer before. Amateur, when I was real young. I started thinking then about starting to carry a camera with me again. To capture that moment.

"AMERICA'S PORT" IS THE TITLE THAT VEST HAS BESTOWED UPON ONE OF HIS FAVORITE PHOTOS; IT IS THE IMAGE HE SHOWS FIRST WHEN GIVING SLIDE SHOWS TO TEACH OUTSIDERS ABOUT THE PORT.

It's a photo of the American flag in sort of an arch over a container ship in the background. And I took it when I was getting off a ship one night. I saw that and I said, "Yeah, that might be a nice photo." I didn't really plan on it. I took about ten photos but this particular one with the arch over the top stood out. And then a couple weeks later, they had some show on television called "America's Port," and it was all about Los Angeles. And I thought, what a bunch of bull. They don't do even a third as many ships as Houston does. And Los Angeles is a Hollywood city. I mean, Houston is a nice working-class city; the Port is central to our economy. Houston's America's port.

Houston is the biggest port in the country. I was talking to a captain at a function for the Maritime Museum. We got to talking about Houston, how much traffic they do, and he said, "Well, I was at a meeting last month, and we had a consultant come in to talk to us about different ports and how we manage traffic and some of the problems we're having. And the consultant had this big dry-erase board, and he starts writing up there, puts up a big circle, and he says, 'Okay, this is Houston, we're going to put this off here by itself for awhile, and then we're going to talk about all these other ports.' And he writes down New York, New Orleans, Los Angeles. And the guy from Los Angeles, he goes, 'Well, how come Houston's separate?' "And the consultant said, 'Well, it's just a different case altogether.' "'No, really. What's so special about Houston?' "And he said, 'Well, how many ships do you do a day over there in Los Angeles?' "He said, 'Well, fifteen, twenty.' "'They're doing seventy ships a day over here. A different case altogether.'"

LOU SEES THE PORT BOTH AS A WORK OF NATURE AND A WORK OF CULTURE. HE VIEWS THE SOCIAL BONDS AND INTERDEPENDENCE OF ITS WORKERS AS AN ORGANIC PHENOMENON, AND THE INDUSTRIAL LANDSCAPE AS ALMOST MAGICAL.

It's an industrial area, but it's not necessarily ugly, I don't think. You know, I always thought I was kind of crazy, because when I was a kid, I remember outside the small town where my grandfather had a ranch, they built a power station, and you could see that power station for miles across the plains in South Texas, and it always looked like a fairy castle to me, with all the lights and the catwalks and the towers. And I thought, "That's kind of cool." And when I grew up, I still had that in my mind.

> There I am with the romance of going to sea: it was like Conrad, Kipling, you know, and I really enjoyed the moment.

And, of course, the Houston Ship Channel, that's all it is: towers and lights. I had two nephews from Colombia; they were from a small town in Colombia. They came up, and we picked them up at the airport. And they were like eight or ten years old, and we're driving over the Beltway 8 bridge, and they're standing up in the car, going, "Wow, look at all the Christmas lights!" you know, and it wasn't: it was just the Port of Houston. The petrochemical complex. But they thought it was beautiful. They thought it was like a crystal palace.

So, to look at it with those eyes is different. So, I'm not going to be all Pollyannaish about it. I mean there's some serious things they do they should probably correct, but they try.

And my experience has been that nobody pollutes deliberately on the Ship Channel that I know of. People make a real effort to keep things clean. When I first started

America's Port is Houston

Photo by Lou Vest

working as a young man, I think the first port I went to was Norfolk—in the Navy as a midshipman. And it was horrible. I mean, the banks of it were like black Crisco, with embedded eggshells and tires, and everything else.

And you don't see that at the Port of Houston. I mean, there's definitely a high tide line and a low tide line, but I think that's as much algae as anything else. You don't see stuff in the water. Now, you will see stuff after a heavy rain. But that's stuff that washes down from Houston. We see islands of trash wash down the Channel from Houston, and it's plastic water bottles and tennis balls and abandoned tennis shoes and tires. And disposable lighters and acres and acres of Styrofoam cups. All that stuff washes down, but that's not thrown overboard by sailors. I'm sure that sailors are not a hundred percent innocent of this, but for the most part, they put their trash away. This is my industrial landscape.

IN THE FOLLOWING PASSAGE, VEST DESCRIBES A PHOTO OF A PILOT ASCENDING A SHIP'S LADDER.

There's a guy jumping onto the pilot boat off the gang-way. I have to say, pilot boat drivers are some of the best boat drivers in the world. You won't find better ship handlers, better boat handlers anywhere than the pilot boat operators. They're very, very good. And you can see in this picture, there's rough sea. They have to bring the pilot boat in next to this ladder and hold it there safely while the guy gets on and off. We do 17,000, 18,000, jobs a year, and these guys are out there bringing these little boats out alongside these ships 17,000, 18,000, times a year, and I've seen them just come up, just as smooth as you could imagine, and put the ladder right within six inches of that gangway there, and you just step across, and they treat it like, "This is what I do every day." And they're good. They're very good. And they should get a lot more credit than they do.

This picture is a metaphor for being a pilot. It's in the middle of the night, and this guy's probably just been woken up about ten minutes before, and he climbs up the ladder, and you can see this stairway going way up there towards the ship, and it's dark at the top. You don't know what's up there. And here's this guy. He probably got up there, and they said, "Okay, you've got your ship coming up." And he goes up there, you know. He doesn't know what kind of crew is up there. He doesn't know if the ship is all in one piece or not. If the engine works right. Is it going to steer well or not? You know, he just goes up there into the darkness, and that's a very good metaphor for a pilot's life.

AT THE END OF HIS INTERVIEW, LOU RETURNED TO THE NOTION OF THE PORT AS AN "ORGANIC ENTITY." HE PORTRAYS PORT LIFE AS THE PRODUCT OF AN INTERDEPENDENT RELATIONSHIP THAT BINDS THE OCEAN TO THE SHIP CHANNEL, AND THE SEAMEN TO THE NATURAL FORCES THAT GIVE THEM THEIR DAILY WORK AND DAILY CHALLENGES.

I think the Port of Houston's a great place. It's been a very exciting place to work—in the best sense, you know. Not that "somebody-screwed-up" sort of exciting. It has been very good to me. And I think what's interesting is I've been impressed by the organic nature of it. How it all works together. All these independent people and agencies: the steamship agents and the terminals. There must be two hundred different docks, and a couple hundred steamship agents, and the Coast Guard, and the Pilots, and the linemen, and the tugboats. And somehow it all comes together to make a big, organic entity. And—like that photo I took of a captain and crew that were smiling—basically, Houston is like that. I mean, there are days when it doesn't function so well, and people get kind of crabby, but thus far it's a well-run, well-organized, happy thing that's trying to do the right, the right thing, for the city and the Port. And I think they deserve recognition: the people who go out to these meetings, and talk about safety, and how to do things better, and how to clean up, and how to prevent accidents. You know, they really seriously try—and the thing organically works very well. ∎

Interview conducted by Carl Lindahl on November 8, 2011
Photo by Margaret Vest

Residence in Magnolia Park
Photo by Neiman Catley

[COMMUNITIES]

HOUSTON IS COMMONLY KNOWN AS A BORDER CITY, the site where the American South meets the Southwest. But there is a third geographic and cultural region that inserts itself into the city's mingled identity: the Gulf Coast. More than any other factor, it is the Ship Channel and the Port of Houston that make the city one with the Gulf.

A look at a map of Texas may easily lead an outsider to wonder how and why Houston could have become a massive port. The Port's headquarters lie more than forty miles from the Gulf, with only the narrow thread of Buffalo Bayou connecting the city to the sea. Houston began as a gateway to the inland West. The city's site was chosen to make it a center for overland transportation. Among the rivers feeding Galveston Bay, Buffalo Bayou is the one that can be navigated farthest west. In the 1800s, boats from the Gulf floated inland to Allen's Landing, and then unloaded their goods onto wagons (and later into railcars) for journeys to San Antonio, Austin, Dallas and beyond. Throughout the nineteenth century Houston's fortunes faced West.

It was the completion of the Ship Channel in 1914 that guaranteed Houston's future as a meeting point of land and sea and tied the city's identity irrevocably to the Gulf. The Ship Channel was the narrow linchpin that coupled Houston with its economic future.

Although it is known around the world as the Port of Houston, the urban complex that lines the Ship Channel represents a constellation of communities with separate identities, roles and histories. Both before and after the Ship Channel opened in 1914, communities sprang up along the banks of Buffalo Bayou. Many of these were distinct towns older than Houston itself, though some were absorbed by Houston as the city spread out toward the sea. Today, Houston is by far the largest of these municipalities, but an understanding of the nature of the Port requires a look at all of them. Each conveys something of the Port's past social composition and present nature.

These communities are home to workers of all kinds who make their living in a trade or industry associated with the Port. Most were founded in the mid to late nineteenth century and grew at the start of the twentieth with the discovery of oil in the region and the onslaught of two world wars. Each had its distinctive beginning: La Porte as a summer residence and amusement mecca; Channelview as the settlement of Lorenzo de Zavala, first vice president of the Republic of Texas; Bayport as the site of one of the original land grants made by Stephen F. Austin and location of the still active Lynchburg Ferry. Pasadena, originally a farming community, still celebrates its past with an annual Strawberry Festival.

The early twentieth century also brought serious work toward the development of the Houston Ship Channel as a waterway to the inland port. The lead-up to the official inauguration of the Port of Houston and the finalized route for the full fifty miles of the Houston Ship Channel created work for skilled and unskilled labor. This, of course, fed the influx of new people to these communities. As the channel was carved from its riverbed, Houston neighborhoods along Buffalo Bayou and the San Jacinto River, as well as the smaller municipalities stretching toward the Gulf, were not only caught up in the work of the port, they also were employed in work on the Port. Residents took on jobs to widen, dredge and clear the channel. And there was constant need for hands to build the docks and warehouses that served the developing channel.

Some of the smaller channel-side communities played especially notable parts in this early history – one remembered now in name only and one still vibrant. Both are now fully ensconced in "Greater Houston". The first, Harrisburg, competed very early on with the city of Houston to be the urban nexus of Texas' gulf coast settlement—even serving for a time as the capital during the period of the Texas Republic. Although Harrisburg's fortunes faded, its comparative proximity to Galveston Bay made it a significant contender to become the channel's endpoint. Ultimately, however, Houston's leaders trumped all other options when they invented the public-private partnership by offering to share the cost of creating the channel with the federal government. Their financial investment and political parlay set the course for the decisive step in situating the head of the channel at the mouth of Buffalo Bayou.

With this outcome, Harrisburg slowly transformed into an industrial hub. Annexed in 1926 by the city of Houston, it is best known nowadays for giving its name to the main artery that crosses

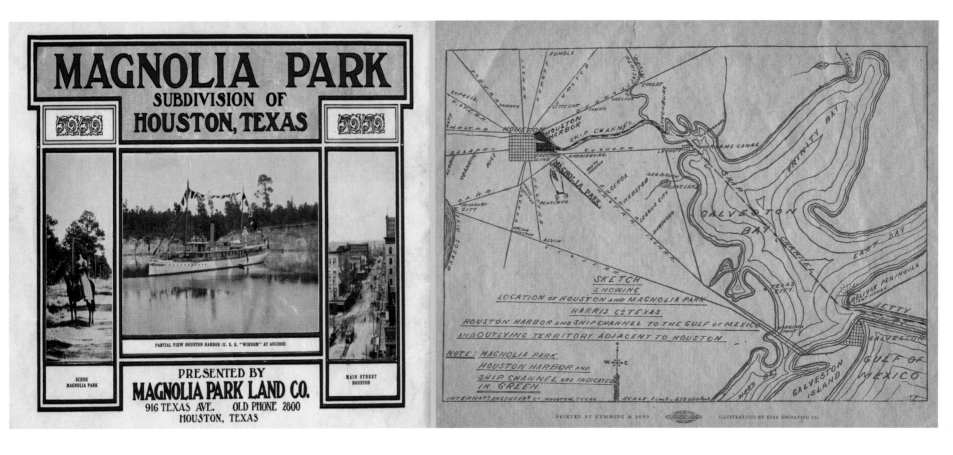

Houston's East End, Harrisburg Boulevard. Like the Allen Brothers before him, John Richardson Harris made a bet on a place and speculated on its possibilities. Unlike the Allen Brothers, his investment failed to pay off as intended. His town was absorbed into the larger city and repurposed to provide the specific industries that serve the Ship Channel. Largely populated now by business headquarters, storage facilities and warehouses, the area that once was the town of Harrisburg has mostly lost its residential character.

Magnolia Park is a mere matter of blocks to the northwest of Harrisburg, just across Braes Bayou. Like Harrisburg, it was once its own separate municipality. Hugging the southern shoal of Buffalo Bayou, it was originally laid out in the 1890s on a plot of land owned by Thomas Brady, but within twenty years or so, the community had become mostly Mexican American. The draw to the area was work, available in the very neighborhood that the families settled. It is no coincidence that the incorporation of Magnolia Park came only one year before the official dedication of the Port of Houston and completion of work on the Houston Ship Channel. By then, it was a coherent and intentional community, in part defined by discriminatory practices that limited Mexican Americans housing opportunities, but also due, in part, to the way in which this early community pushed back against prejudice by creating a robust social, economic and cultural life for itself. Schools, churches, and social and fraternal organizations grew up during this period and to this day continue to play a part in this still vital neighborhood.

LEFT : Advertisement for Magnolia Park Subdivision of Houston, Texas. *Courtesy of Houston Public Library, HMRC: MSS0118*

RIGHT : Map of Magnolia Park and the Houston Ship Channel. *Courtesy of Houston Public Library, HMRC: MSS0118*

Adolph Postel, one of the first Mexican Americans employed as an engineer on the Port Terminal Railroad, was born ten blocks away from the Turning Basin in 1927. His parents had come from Victoria, Texas to Magnolia Park, where his father immediately found work as a longshoreman. His brothers worked on the docks. He too started out there and even went to sea for a while. But eventually, in 1951, Postel found employment doing unskilled work with the Port Terminal Railroad. At this time, Mexican Americans were relegated to positions with less responsibility and lower pay. Postel remembers: "Way back then, the Latinos just worked the dirty work. [There was a] lot of discrimination against the Latinos, [but] mostly against the blacks." However, in 1970, likely in response to political activity on the part of activist groups in the Mexican American community[1], questions were asked about the apportionment of jobs throughout the industries associated with the Port. Postel was promoted to engineer and remained in that position until his retirement in 1989. He is quick to say: "It got better and better. There are quite a few [Latinos] running locomotives now. It is a good paying job, one of the better paying jobs [and] a good pension." He and his family live to this day in Magnolia Park.

Residences in Magnolia Park.
Photos by Neiman Catley

The next generation benefited from the struggles of their parents and grandparents. Gilda Ramirez, who grew up in her grandparents' home in Magnolia Park, notes how absolutely central the Port was in the economic life of the community.

[1] Mexican American Youth Organization, the Raza Unida party and the Mexican American Legal Defense and Education Fund

I would venture to say that every single person that grew up in the Magnolia Park area is somehow tied to the Port Authority, whether they worked at the Port or at a convenience store along Navigation [Boulevard]. I remember the Italian families that lived here—the Carrabas and the Mandolas. I remember Johnny Carraba and Rosie Carraba—who sold their restaurants but still have the original one on Kirby—they had a small family-owned convenience store on Canal Street. We would go there often and I remember that during lunch all of these men with hard hats and steel toe shoes would come in. Rosie would always make sandwiches, hot dogs and barbecue sandwiches and they would sell out. All of the workers from the Port would come in and they always had the smell of oil or pipe and steel on them.

And as time went on, the opportunities afforded by the Port for workers to make a better living for themselves and, eventually to advance in their careers, meant that their children and grandchildren saw even greater progress. Ramirez, who is a member of the Port of Houston Authority leadership today, makes her family's upward social motion a poignant part of her remembrance:

...a lot of second- and third-generation workers have been able to send their children to college. We often laugh because my father worked on the docks and I get to look out of my window and see the docks from my office.

Magnolia Park's development into a coherent Mexican American community and enclave has an almost organic feel to it. The increased migration of Mexican Americans to the city during this period coincided with the Port's earliest years and the location *enhanced* its attractiveness as a residential destination. The story of Clinton Park, however, is a different one. While its proximity to Galena Park and to Clinton Avenue made it a logical residential option for workers on the north side of the Houston Ship Channel, it was developed in direct response to Jim Crow laws forbidding residential integration. Next door to Galena Park, Clinton Park was developed after World War II specifically to house African Americans. Even when the two cities shared streets, barriers were erected to cut them off from each other. Despite these stifling legal restrictions, families were able to participate with pride in the great American dream of home ownership. Van Chatman, a third generation longshoreman whose grandfather plied the same trade, notes:

My grandfather lived in Clinton Park. A lot of workers from the Ship Channel bought those houses. African Americans came into these communities and lived in them and prospered in them. It was an old traditional community, a nice community that gave people self-esteem. In my opinion, longshoremen didn't create it, but the community was able to sustain and keep the longshoreman families close to the job, and they ended up being mainstays to these communities. Clinton Park wasn't the only one—Pleasantville and Clinton View were adjacent communities.

Houston Monarchs
vs
Southern Pacific
t End Park
8 ~ 8th 1926
City Champions.

1472
Schlueter
Houston
Tex

Clinton Park today is not the community that Van Chatman describes—integration changed all that—but it gave middle class black families a real property-based foothold in the city and a visibility from which there was no turning back as the 1950s became the 1960s and civil rights were on the table day in and day out. And as Chatman says, there were similar communities that grew up around the port and as a result of the port. In their shared interview, Homer Guillory and Joseph Kinch underscore the importance of these communities and their identities as African American strongholds in the city. These neighborhoods were tightly interconnected. Describing some of the ways in which workers organized during difficult times, and especially during the big strike of 1968, Guillory was quick to use an example:

> *The black community surrounds the Port of Houston. From Galena Park, Pleasantville, Fifth Ward, Acres Home, going back to Sunnyside, word spread like fire. The whole labor force would get word and the word was —we were gonna do the right thing.* ∎

FATHER RIVERS
PATOUT

THE *very* FIRST DAYS WE OPENED, *people* *came* IN DROVES

HERE THE LATE FATHER RIVERS PATOUT (1938-2014) TELLS THE INSIDE STORY OF AN INSTITUTION CENTRAL TO THE PORT OF HOUSTON AND ITS SHIP CHANNEL. FATHER PATOUT WAS A CHAPLAIN AT THE HOUSTON INTERNATIONAL SEAFARERS' CENTER, A BUILDING PERCHED ON THE CHANNEL'S TURNING BASIN, CLOSE BY THE HEADQUARTERS OF THE PORT OF HOUSTON AUTHORITY. THE SEAFARERS' CENTER WAS BUILT TO SERVE THE MEN AND WOMEN WHO WORK ON THE DOCKS AND IN THE INDUSTRIES THAT LINE THE CHANNEL, OR WHO ARRIVE ON THE SHIPS THAT TRANSPORT THE REMARKABLE AMOUNT OF TONNAGE THAT MOVES IN AND OUT OF HOUSTON ANNUALLY. IT IS BY NO MEANS A PREPOSSESSING BUILDING BUT, LIKE THE HUMAN HEART, THE MUSCULARITY OF ITS MISSION IS UNDENIABLE.

A NATIVE TEXAN, FATHER PATOUT WAS THERE FROM THE CENTER'S INCEPTION, A YOUNG PRIEST FULL OF THE VIGOR AND SOCIAL VISION THAT INFUSED THE CATHOLIC CHURCH IN THE MID-1960S.

THROUGH HIS LONG TENURE AND CONTINUED DEDICATION TO SERVING SEAFARERS, HE WITNESSED THE CHANGE IN THE CONDITIONS AND CHARACTER OF THE WORK CONDUCTED AT THE PORT OF HOUSTON. MOST OF ALL, HE CAME TO KNOW THE SEA-FARER COMMUNITY ITSELF: ITS CHALLENGES AND TRIALS, ITS ASSETS AND STRENGTHS. WHETHER THEY AGREED WITH HIM OR NOT, FEW WOULD DENY THAT HE WAS ONE OF ITS GREATEST AND MOST VOCAL ADVOCATES.

I was ordained in 1967—over the time when the Vatican II was happening. My very first assignment was down near the port at a place called Blessed Sacrament and that's where we got to find out about seafarers. Serving seafarers was a very big social concern. In 1968 we came to this port to start ministering to seafarers and we borrowed a building from the St. Vincent de Paul on Harrisburg, a number of miles to the south—upstairs, hot—but the very first days we opened, people came in droves walking up to these areas and we said, "We must have something right here."

Our first presumption was, "Why would seafarers ever want a priest or minister telling them they couldn't read Playboy or drink beer?" What a stereotype! That was a common stereotype, still today, that they are alcoholic womanizers. On the contrary, it was very evident soon that they found they were family people, great people and, in fact, they taught us that they were probably some of the more tolerant people in the world because they had seen every culture and didn't hold it against you to be of particular religion or race—that there were good and bad of all kinds.

FATHER PATOUT WORKED HAND-IN-HAND WITH SOME OF THE CITY'S MOST NOTED LEADERS TO MAKE THE WORK OF SERVING SEAFARERS MORE THAN A MINISTRY. ESTABLISHING A SITE AND ORGANIZING A BUILDING CAMPAIGN CALLED FOR A BROAD CONSORTIUM OF INTERESTS AND A PRAGMATIC SENSE OF MUTUALITY BETWEEN SOCIAL CONCERNS AND BUSINESS INTERESTS.

In those early years, we were very, very fortunate to have people who really took an interest. We had a number of socialites and our churches, but I would say Howard Tellepsen—who was at that time head of the Port Commission—was probably more important than anyone else because he made a commitment to build a building with his company and raised the funds we didn't have through his foundation—what an offer!

The first president was Albert Leidis. He was a Belgian captain and he was a hard-drinking, fussing and cussing person and he had seen the deprivations of the seafarers on the ships in his early days when they were fed terrible food and under restrictions. And he really believed that seafarers needed a better life. I really credit him with being the founder of the Center's idea here and he'd gotten permission to get land for where we built the building, but he didn't have any money. So when we came in with money, it was a great marriage.

And even the different philosophies—there was always a little tension between the business people and the social helpers [that were part of our Board] because they didn't want the business slowed down. But again, it was a wonderful tension that helped us to look at both sides of the situation. How can we have a beautiful center to help people? How can we help the Port to have better efficiency?

> [*...it was very evident soon that they found they were family people, great people and, in fact, they taught us that they were probably some of the more tolerant people in the world*]

RATHER THAN ACCEPT THE RECEIVED MODEL OF HOW SUCH AN INSTITUTION MIGHT WORK, THE FOUNDERS DECIDED TO TAKE AN INTERNATIONALIST, ECUMENICAL APPROACH TO DEVELOPING THE CENTER. IT WAS A SIMPLE BUT REVOLUTIONARY STEP.

I'd taken my vacation that summer to go out to the West Coast to visit a couple of seafarer centers and asked them what was right. So we built a seafarer's center here in Houston, the very first in the world, none had ever been done before, that shared all the interests of each of the denominations, shared the business, shared the poor. Every other center up until that time had to be either built by a particular church or particular national government.

So we were the pioneers on that and thank You, Lord, it was a great thing. Now this is the model for the world. And nowadays seafarers are diverse on every ship and that just makes more sense than ever—that they can come here without being asked, "What do you believe? Where are you from?" Our model spread throughout the world.

BUT IN ADDITION TO FURTHERING THE WORK OF CHAPLAINS LIKE FATHER PATOUT AND HIS ASSOCIATES, THE CENTER'S FACILITIES WERE KEY TO BETTERING THE PHYSICAL AND MENTAL WELFARE OF THE SEAFARERS WHO UTILIZED IT. SPORTS FACILITIES PROVIDED RESPITE FROM THE CONFINES OF A SHIP, ENTERTAINMENT AND AN OPPORTUNITY FOR SAILORS AND WORKERS OF ALL NATIONALITIES TO CONNECT WITH EACH OTHER.

We first opened in a building some miles away; it was borrowed—but under construction was a swimming pool, the soccer field and the track. We started using those in about two years. Meanwhile, the building was under construction and, finally, when it opened in 1973, we knew a lot more about how to be chaplains to seafarers.

The athletic program was very important in the early days—we had sports week and the winning ship got these big trophies and prizes and there was a dance and a big hoopla. So it was very active in the early days. We had one or two games every night. We have uniforms we'd give them. We even have shoes that were donated. Sometimes, we had rivalry between the two ships; sometimes we bring a local team out to play. [It was] very active in the early days because they had time and they had people and they had young people!

I never will forget we had a tournament once at our festival and some girls were playing on one of the teams and beat the ones with the Greeks. And they were just furious, throwing chairs, "How could you let women do this?" But it was a very active participation in the early days and very fun.

I remember one of the interesting events was Chinese sailors who wanted to go swimming. And we had one of those little shacks for a change room, but they didn't speak English and so our volunteers would kind of point to the basket, and would hand them their clothes and then point to the shack. Well, these Chinese sailors bowed solemnly, took off all their clothes right in front of the volunteers, bowed again and put the swimming suits on.

LIKE THE BALANCING OF BUSINESS AND SOCIAL CONCERNS, DEVELOPING THE SINGLE INTERNATIONAL CENTER AVOIDED DUPLICATION BUT MAXIMIZED INTERACTION AMONG THE DIVERSE RELIGIOUS AND NATIONAL COMMUNITIES. THIS APPROACH CONTRIBUTED TO HEIGHTENED UNDERSTANDING AND TOLERANCE BUT OFTEN CALLED FOR FORBEARANCE AND DIPLOMACY.

We try to be open and helpful. We don't proselytize. That's why the chapel is separated here so that when there is a chapel service, those go that choose to go. The bar doesn't close down, the music doesn't stop. And it's worked out wonderful over the years. I want to tell you one ecumenical story. When we were in our early years, we said, "We want this chapel to welcome people of different faiths." And for Islam, they face east. They get the prayer rug, and they pray their prayers on the prayer rug and so we had a prayer rug donated and I said, "Isn't that wonderful, let's go put it in the chapel. And find out where East is." I deliberately went out when I was going start the mass and asked some of these Islamic people to please come. Well, they're sitting in there dutifully and I'm standing in front of them saying, "Now, in respect to your religion, we have got this prayer rug, and here is east, we want you to come and use this for your prayers whenever you feel." They weren't smiling, they were kind of frowning. And so one of them started to get up and, later on, I found out what an offense it was to stay with your shoes on the prayer rug. You learn a lot about those things. So, these are things they taught us over the years.

> *How can we have a beautiful center to help people? How can we help the Port to have better efficiency?*

I have a favorite story. This was the Cold War and the Russians definitely did not want their seafarers to be influenced by capitalism and Western things. So they all had a commissar aboard who is in charge of politi-

cal thought. So we had to be very careful—one was the bibles; it would be against the rules for them to take bibles. Therefore, we put plain brown covers on them. And when the commissar wasn't looking they knew when to take them. We wouldn't take them aboard ship.

But one of my favorite stories is about Christmas. I went aboard one ship and I said to the commissar, "I have brought New Year's gifts." They weren't Christmas gifts then because Christmas is a Christian holiday. But they celebrate New Year's and I said, "I want to bring them aboard for you. They're made by the people of this community and they want to share it with you."

"Nyet." [Said the commissar], who looked like a World War II veteran with his pockmarks, and his big moustache, and his Russian cigarettes. And so, the captain was sitting here. He wanted the presents. But the commissar wasn't sure. And they finally said, "Well, can we see one?" I said [whispers] "Please let there be no bible in it."

So we opened up one: combs, socks, writing paper. And they said, "Well, we can't accept because we don't have a gift to you." And I said, "Well, I'll take a drink of vodka, you know," and the captain smiling said, "Well, we don't have vodka but we just came back from Cuba and we got some great Cuban rum." And I said, "Okay." So we go upstairs now to the captain's office and the commissar [is] wearily looking, he doesn't like what's developing.

So we said, "Toast to the American seafarers, toast to the Russian seafarers, toast to the friendship of all that gather." And each one toasted and after a few toasts they said, "Okay, we'll take the gift." I said, "Nyet, not the gift, a gift for everybody. Toast to the American seafarers, toast to the Russian seafarers." By this time it has been toasted enough. So they've agreed, finally. The commissar's defeated philosophically, so we get the presents, put them on aboard. And I'm having a little trouble navigating down the gangway and as I was about to leave I said "Happy New Year!" And the captain looks

around, "Merry Christmas!" It was a political game, you know, but that was very significant in the early days.

[
So we said, "Toast to the American seafarers, toast to the Russian seafarers, toast to the friendship of all that gather."
]

FROM THE DAY THE SEAFARERS' CENTER WAS FINISHED—FOR AS WELL RECEIVED AND LAUDED AS IT WAS, FOR AS MUCH AS ANY LOCAL WORKER OR INTERNATIONAL SEAFARER ENJOYED ITS EXTRAS AND ITS AMENITIES—IT FACED OBSOLESCENCE. THE CHARACTER OF THE WORK THAT SEAFARERS PERFORMED WAS CHANGING; THE NUMBER OF WORKERS NEEDED WAS SHRINKING.

In the early days, it would be ordinary to have two hundred people a night up. I didn't have eleven people last night. Now, we do a lot of work. We provided the Wi-Fi so they could use their computer on the ship. We provided telephones. We provided other aids to help them but the number of people coming in to the Center—I think the biggest night we had recently was fifty-eight, because the church was putting on a party and they came to that. So, that's a great night today.

In the early days, that would have been a terrible night. The big center like this—we don't need the space—we need more mobile transportation, we need more aboard-the-ship presence. The ministry is alive and well and the Seafarers' Center is alive and well and helping people but in terms of the types of help, it's different from when we started.

We would not have the large numbers of people and the swimming pool—which is fantastic—and those who come really love it. But again, the swimming pool would be full every night too. We had to hire a lifeguard. We don't do that anymore but we would probably get the most use out of the basketball court, the Ping-Pong table, the pool tables, but even those things are not utilized in the way they had been before.

The biggest change, of course, is the time in port and the number of people on a ship. When I started, forty was an average aboard a ship. Now, twenty, if you're lucky, is an average aboard a ship. They'd be here a week—they get time to socialize, time to work, time to get their shopping done. Today, two days is a long time in port, and many would leave on the same day they come in.

CONTAINERIZATION AND TECHNOLOGY CONTINUE TO ALTER THE WORKPLACE AND THE KIND AND QUALITY OF WORKERS THAT FIND THEIR WAY TO THE PORT AND SHIP CHANNEL. TODAY THE WORK AND THE WORKER HARDLY RESEMBLE THE PLACE AND THE PEOPLE THE CENTER WAS BUILT TO SERVE.

So, everything is speeded up. [Now] we would never build this Center with all these beautiful things. We haven't played soccer in the soccer field in years. You know, eleven people that can get off at any one time, that would be over half the crew, and they're older because there's seniority. And there's less women because they were brought in when they had need of more seafarers. They were excluded when they didn't, because they were the last ones in.

Technology, technology—you know, we had a lot of backbreaking jobs, you had to pull this pulley and lift that bale and upload aboard. Now, it's all done automatically. You don't need to have a radio operator aboard. You couldn't even sail the ship when I came unless you have a radio operator that can do all the communications. No such thing exists anymore. You just turn your computer on and you use satellite guiding and you push a button and it does the things that you used to have to do by hand. And the economics of it all: "We need to reduce crews to reduce costs." "We're going to be competitive." Containers, you know—used to be everything came in bulk and had to be unloaded individually.

Now, you just have to lift the box out and no human is doing it. It's a big crane lifting them out. You can clear a container ship in a day and you can roll-off 5,000 automobiles in a day on a Ro-Ro ramp. Most of the things are so automated that you don't need the personnel and you don't need the time to do that. It's part of the speed of the moving in and out of the Port because the ship is working all the time in port, that's their hardest work. When they're at sea, they can actually rest a little bit but here in port, they have to take on supply; they have to load and unload; they have to repair anything that needs repairing. And so, they are busy aboard ship.

> *Technology, technology—you know, we had a lot of backbreaking jobs, you had to pull this pulley and lift that bale and upload aboard. Now, it's all done automatically.*

AND NOW HOMELAND SECURITY PROVISIONS RESULTING FROM THE 9/11 ATTACKS HAVE COMPLETELY REARRANGED THE LANDSCAPE OF THE PORT OF HOUSTON AND THE HOUSTON SHIP CHANNEL.

The worst possible thing that could have happened to seafarers is Homeland Security. The restrictions are so horrible—having to get visas in their own country before they're even allowed to consider getting off [the ship] and they're very expensive visas. The restrictions when they get here—they're inspected ninety-six hours out to sea for any possible connection to terrorism. Then they're boarded by the Coast Guard and looked at and examined again when they're docked in. And when they're docked, Immigration goes again and checks each one of them. If they don't have the documentation, they cannot leave their ship. But even if they have the documentation, it's often the facility that makes it very difficult. We have people having to pay a couple hundred dollars to go a couple hundred yards from the ship to the gate, each way. You know, that's just horrible and an ordinary seafarer cannot afford that. I'm on a dock access committee

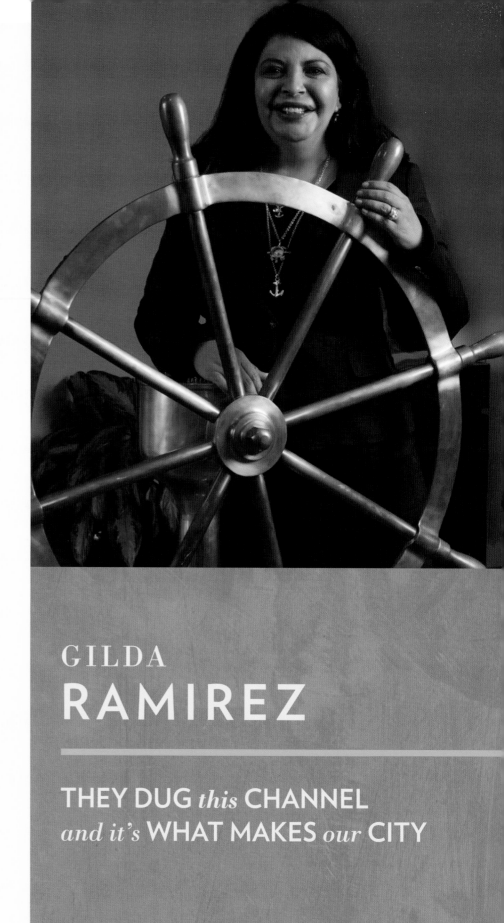

for the Coast Guard and our job is to guarantee that any seafarer that has permission to leave should be able to leave without cost and come back without cost to board the ship.

If you were a worker coming in, you have to have a TWIC [Transportation Worker Identification Credential] card. If you're a seafarer—American—you have to have one; now, foreigners can't own one. But even an American stationed right below our Center can look up there and see the Center, he can't walk up to the Center anymore, unless somebody like myself with a TWIC and an escort card picks him up, brings him up and takes him back. So freedom of movement is horribly restricted. These are some of the real changes that have happened since 9/11. ▌

Interview conducted by Pat Jasper on July 26, 2010.
©Houston Chronicle/Nick de la Torre. Used with permission.

GILDA
RAMIREZ

THEY DUG *this* CHANNEL
and it's WHAT MAKES *our* CITY

THERE IS A CERTAIN PRIDE IN BEING FROM MAGNOLIA PARK. ASK GILDA RAMIREZ, A NATIVE HOUSTONIAN AND PORT OF HOUSTON AUTHORITY EMPLOYEE, AND SHE WILL VIVIDLY DESCRIBE A THRIVING NEIGHBORHOOD THAT HAS ALWAYS BEEN INTERTWINED WITH THE PORT OF HOUSTON. IN THESE EXCERPTS FROM AN INTERVIEW, GILDA RAMIREZ GIVES US INSIGHT INTO HER FAMILY'S CONNECTION TO THE PORT. SHE RECOUNTS THE SIGHTS AND SMELLS OF HER CHILDHOOD NEIGHBORHOOD CLOSE TO THE HOUSTON SHIP CHANNEL AND REMINISCES ABOUT WATCHING THE PORT GROW AND PROSPER.

Most of the families in Magnolia Park were somehow tied to the Port Authority in direct or indirect jobs. I recognized that as a child. You would see truck parts or machinery and you knew that those things were coming across the docks. It has just been a blessing to our family to be a part of Houston and the Port Authority and to watch the growth and the prosperity and the jobs that the Port generates.

I had exposure to the Port very early on. Some of my earliest memories were from when I was four or five years old, coming to the Port Authority and picking up uncles or brothers when they were clearing customs and were coming home from the trips abroad. A lot of my family members made their livelihoods through the Port of Houston Authority. Growing up in Magnolia Park, you were somewhat limited as to different types of cultures that you would see, but because our family worked at the Port, we would look forward to the gifts that we would get from around the world.

I remember, as a child, the smell of oil and I associated that smell with making a living, and having money. The port workers would come back on Friday and they always had a roll of cash. So I always associated that smell with a job and money. I guess it was black oil. I remember several of our neighbors walking to the corner, getting in a truck and carpooling to the Port Authority and then coming back in the evening and their wives waiting outside for their spouses. I remember my mother and other people making lunch for the workers in the big lunch pails that

they would carry. So it's funny to associate the smells with the work and with the hustle and bustle and movement of the Port Authority. I remember knowing that they had to have really hearty meals because they had to work as hard as they did.

> *..., you were somewhat limited as to different types of cultures that you would see, but because our family worked at the Port, we would look forward to the gifts that we would get from around the world.*

MAGNOLIA BEGAN AS AN ANGLO SETTLEMENT IN THE 1890S, BELONGING TO THOMAS M. BRADY. BEGINNING IN 1911, A SIGNIFICANT NUMBER OF MEXICAN AMERICAN LABORERS SETTLED THERE, IN WHAT WAS THEN AN INDEPENDENT MUNICIPALITY. THESE WORKERS, WHO HAILED MOSTLY FROM SOUTH TEXAS, HELPED LAY RAILROAD TRACKS, DREDGED AND WIDENED THE BUFFALO BAYOU, LOADED COTTON ON SHIPS AND RAILROAD CARS AND HELPED CONSTRUCT THE SHIP CHANNEL[1]. AS THE COMMUNITY GREW IT CAME TO BE KNOWN AS ONE OF THE OLDEST LATINO NEIGHBORHOODS IN HOUSTON, AND BY 1929 IT WAS ONE OF THE LARGEST.

LIKE THE REST OF THE NATION, THE GENERAL HOUSTON POPULATION EXPERIENCED AN UPWARD MOBILITY DUE TO THE WAR-RELATED ECONOMIC OPPORTUNITIES OF THE 1940S. BUT BY THE 1960S, THE BULK OF MAGNOLIA PARK'S MEXICAN AMERICAN RESIDENTS REMAINED WORKING CLASS. GILDA REMEMBERS HARD TIMES AND THE STRATEGIES HER FAMILY USED TO COPE WITH ECONOMIC DIFFICULTIES. ONE SUCH STRATEGY WAS HER FATHER'S PARTICIPATION IN THE INTERNATIONAL LONGSHOREMEN'S ASSOCIATION.

When I was born, my grandfather was already retired, but the stories that the family told were about him coming home dirty and tired. He would sometimes bring back

[1] Diana J. Kleiner, "MAGNOLIA PARK, TX," Handbook of Texas Online (http://www.tshaonline.org/handbook/online/articles/hvm06), accessed March 06, 2014.

sacks of potatoes or sacks of onions that came across the docks. Before containerization, if a bag busted there were things that people could take, legally of course, or buy at a discount. I can remember the stories of how we would get potatoes and we were able to make our food go further. During those times, having nine children was very, very difficult.

My father was a member of the International Longshoremen's Association. He and another family member would strategize and invite other members to participate. They were concerned, even then, about their pensions and their hourly rates and how they were going to make ends meet and what they needed to do—not just for themselves, but for others—and to make sure that they were being paid fairly. I think the union has always been a really good partner with everyone in this community. They have worked hand-in-hand ensuring that everyone's rights were addressed and that workers received the best available pay and that they were taken care of and had a safe place to work.

> [The Union has] worked hand-in-hand ensuring that everyone's rights were addressed and that workers received the best available pay and that they were taken care of and had a safe place to work.

WHILE THE MAJORITY OF THE NEIGHBORHOOD WAS LATINO, RESIDENTS ALSO DEVELOPED UNIQUE RELATIONSHIPS WITH PEOPLE OF VARIOUS CULTURAL AND SOCIOECONOMIC BACKGROUNDS TO CREATE AN INTERDEPENDENT NETWORK OF NEIGHBORS, CO-WORKERS, CLIENTS, TENANTS AND LANDLORDS.

I would venture to say that every single person that grew up in the Magnolia Park area is somehow tied to the Port Authority, whether they worked at the Port or at a convenience store along Navigation [Boulevard]. I remember the Italian families that lived here—the Carrabas and the Mandolas. I remember Johnny Carraba and Rosie Carraba—who sold their restaurants but still have the original one on Kirby—they had a small family owned convenience store on Canal Street. We would go there often and I remember that during lunch all of these men with hard hats and steel-toe shoes would come in. Rosie would always make sandwiches—hot dogs and barbecue sandwiches—and they would sell out. All of the workers from the Port would come in and they always had the smell of oil or pipe and steel on them. I love to say that that's where I had my first credit card.

> I remember, as a child, the smell of oil and I associated that smell with making a living, and having money.

The Carrabas had an honor system and my parents had a little account there. You could go in and buy something and at the end of the week, when your father got paid, he would go in and pay your bills. That was really our first line of credit, if you will. Those families were also part of the whole Magnolia Park effort and movement. They were very supportive and it was interesting because they were Italian and almost everyone else was Hispanic. There was also an Asian grocery store as well. Because it was near a port, there was an Asian grocery store, an Italian grocery store and a Greek restaurant, and so we did develop a flavor for all of the different types of foods.

AS NEW GENERATIONS WORKED THE PORT, THERE EMERGED A MIDDLE CLASS THAT WAS ABLE TO SEND SUBSEQUENT GENERATIONS TO COLLEGE. MANY OF THOSE IMMIGRANTS, INCLUDING GILDA, MOVED OUT OF THEIR CHILDHOOD NEIGHBORHOODS BUT ULTIMATELY RETURNED TO THE AREA WHERE THEY GREW UP, HOUSTON'S EAST END.

Two of my grandfather's sons, my father, my uncle and my brothers worked on the docks. One was a Merchant Marine, and when he would go out of the country and go on these journeys, he would send all of his money to his family and because of that they were able to purchase houses. They became landlords and were able to reap the benefits of owning property and renting houses for extra income. They always rented to other people who would leave here and go to different areas. I remember they would go to California and Detroit. They were migrant workers who worked the fields. So the family always rented at lower than market value to these people who were also involved in the same type of industry. After all, the food that those workers harvested had to be transported back to this area. So the touch of the Port is very widespread and it impacts everyone's lives and livelihoods.

It's a great story. This neighborhood has flourished and people have been able to move on, a lot of second- and third-generation workers have been able to send their children to college. We often laugh because my father worked on the docks, and I get to look out of my window and see the docks from my office. So all of his hard work and the fruits of his labor have definitely paid off. I've lived in the area for most of my life. I love the area and am so glad to see the resurgence that is occurring. I can't wait to see what new development we will see in the East End.

> *This neighborhood has flourished and people have been able to move on, a lot of second- and third-generation workers have been able to send their children to college.*

I believe that the Port is very important to the history of our city. The Ship Channel was constructed with the foresight of our forefathers; they dug this Channel and it's what makes our city today. ▮

Interview conducted by Pat Jasper on June 8, 2012.
Photo by Loriana Espinel.

VAN
CHATMAN

A *Longshoreman's* LEGACY

VAN CHATMAN IS A THIRD-GENERATION LONGSHOREMAN. HIS STORIES AND EXPERIENCES POINT TO THE WAYS IN WHICH WATERFRONT WORK HAS PRESENTED BOTH OPPORTUNITIES AND DIFFICULTIES TO AFRICAN AMERICANS ASPIRING TO UPWARD MOBILITY. HE BEGINS WITH HIS GRANDFATHER'S STORY:

My grandfather migrated from Louisiana in the 1930s. He met some guys who were working on the docks. They spoke a French dialect, so he was able to become "one of the guys." At the time, there was no knowledge of when the ships would come in. The guys would meet and play dominoes and pool in a private area where they would entertain themselves until the ships came in. He was a cotton worker, which was one of the highest paying jobs. He would work it here in Houston and when the cotton would leave here he would go work at other ports like Corpus and Brownsville. He was committed to following the trade. My grandfather was one of the first to get retirement with benefits, including hospitalization.

I was able to see him when he was a younger guy, but after all those years of working cotton, he walked around with a walker. He couldn't get around and had chronic arthritis. I can understand the sacrifice my grandfather made, but at the end of the day, he wasn't upset about it all. He was a jolly, nice guy with a quiet demeanor. He had other scars from it too. Even though he made good money, he had a lot of social problems with the family. It was hard to keep the family happy while he was traveling to different cities. He made some good points—it doesn't matter how successful a person is, it's the small things that really count. As he got older, he was more into the family that he didn't get to spend a lot of time with. He was a little saddened by that.

THE PRESENCE OF AFRICAN AMERICANS ON HOUSTON'S DOCKS WAS COMMONPLACE EARLY ON. COMMUNITIES TO HOUSE THEM FOLLOWED. CHATMAN'S GRANDFATHER RESIDED IN AN AREA KNOWN FOR BEING AN EARLY HOME TO BLACK WORKERS WHEN HOUSING SEGREGATION WAS STANDARD THROUGHOUT THE UNITED STATES. WHAT WAS NOT SO COMMON FOR AFRICAN AMERICANS WAS HOME OWNERSHIP. THE OPPORTUNITIES ASSOCIATED WITH THE HOUSTON SHIP CHANNEL AND WORK AS A LONGSHOREMAN MADE THIS POSSIBLE FOR MANY.

My grandfather lived in Clinton Park. We would go there for visits and talk to him and his wife. I would visit my grandfather often. Clinton Park was one of the first communities for African Americans that had subdivisions. It was very neat and had clean neighborhoods and people kept up their yards and their houses. A lot of workers from the Ship Channel bought those houses. African Americans came into these communities and lived in them and prospered in them. It was an old traditional community, a nice community that gave people self-esteem. In my opinion, longshoremen didn't create it, but the community was able to sustain and keep the longshoreman families close to the job and they ended up being mainstays to these communities. Clinton Park wasn't the only one—Pleasantville and Clinton View were adjacent communities.

The waterfront allowed African Americans to live a life that was unheard of, so far as being able to buy homes. You had a credit union here to get loans. My grandfather was living like any other American at that time. He was making the economic transition to be included in American society as a citizen and a taxpayer, but it was grueling work. My grandfather spoke about witnessing people getting killed doing cotton work, lines breaking on the winches, and snatching blocks coming loose. He witnessed some people losing their lives; that's how dangerous the work was. He was a fair guy and a law-abiding person. He taught me work ethic. We were just like any other person in America; we could go and buy the clothes that we wanted to buy, but I didn't really know how hard he was working. Growing up from that to my first day on the waterfront was a rude awakening.

The unspoken testimony here is that you're talking about Houston when segregation was still going on. At that time, there was a transition. The rest of the country was integrating and this was one of the last areas that was forced to integrate, back in 1983. I remember going on ships where one part of the ship was [worked by] whites and the other was [worked by] blacks. It was acceptable.

Nobody questioned it—that was just "the way it was." They did have water fountains that were colored-only but, I think, it was such a close-knit community that it was about making money. At that particular time, it was acceptable as a way of life. You were not there to question it; you were there to make money.

> The waterfront allowed
> African Americans to
> live a life that was unheard of,
> so far as being able to buy homes.

THE FIRST-GENERATION OF WATERFRONT WORKERS OFTEN PAVED THE WAY FOR THE NEXT. VAN CHATMAN'S FATHER WAS ABLE TO FORGE AN INROAD IN THIS MANNER BUT HE WAS SURPRISED WHEN HE DISCOVERED THAT HIS SON HAD THE SAME IMPULSE.

My grandfather was a top seniority guy. My dad ended up being a foreman. My dad worked a lot of cotton as well. He wasn't a big guy like my grandfather was, so he trucked cotton. You didn't have to be big to work cotton, but most of the guys were physical specimens, just huge, strong guys. That was before forklifts. My dad would tell me stories about when the first forklifts arrived on the docks. People would say, "Don't get on these forklifts; they're going to take jobs away from us." My dad was one of the first guys on one because he said, "Hey, this is going to make my job easier." It evolved from being afraid of automation, to accepting it. One day, he asked me what I wanted to do. I said, "Hey Dad, I want to be a longshoreman like you." I will never forget his expression. He stopped what he was doing and his whole demeanor changed. He said, "You don't want to do that; this is hard work. You stay in school, you hear me?" I didn't really know—people make this job look easy, but it's a very, very tough job.

ALTHOUGH CHATMAN'S FATHER WOULD HAVE PREFERRED THAT THE YOUNGER CHATMAN FIND OTHER WORK, THE WATERFRONT AFFORDED A SIGNIFICANT LEVEL OF PAY AND BENEFITS AT A TIME WHEN FEW SUCH WERE AVAILABLE TO YOUNG AFRICAN AMERICAN MEN. VAN CHATMAN DISCUSSES THE DIFFERENT KINDS OF WORK HE WAS ENGAGED IN.

I have worked loading 110 to 120-pound sacks to coffee drums, which can weigh as much as 800 pounds. I have been a truck driver. I have worked containers. Industry has gone from handwork to mostly containers. Some of the work is physical and some of it is more skill-based, where you are driving machinery. There were some times when other people would come out, people like football players. It was funny because we would watch them quit at twelve o'clock. We weren't athletes, we were just used to it. It wasn't so physical as you would think; a lot of it was mental and a lot of tricks to the trade, knowing how not to lift dead weight. You would be surprised that someone small in stature could actually have the ability to work sacks. Most of us have bad backs. It comes with the territory if you are not lifting properly. If you do that consistently, you will work against your body structure. I guess over time, your body does learn to deal with it and strengthen itself. At the same time, once you get used to that, you can't just go and get another type of employment. It doesn't work totally. So, you actually get conditioned to this. We have people who leave here and come back years later and say, "I never should have left."

It takes pride. That's something that was taught to us by the old-timers. The slogan was, "A fair day's work for a fair day's pay." Previous longshoremen worked much, much harder than we did. There wasn't any machinery. They pushed cargo by hand. It was a lot of cotton work—really backbreaking work. They paved the way for us and our benefits. There wasn't even retirement. My dad told me that guys would work until they couldn't work anymore and then they would just show up on the docks and guys would pitch in and give them money. That was

retirement. At some point, they created a job where they would hand out water and would be hired as part of the working gang. That was to help old-timers who couldn't do the physical work. As you get older, you have to elevate yourself from the actual manual labor. You learn another skill after sweating it hard for thirty years. I have obtained seniority.

The Port has always been available to people for a second chance at life, and first chance as well. We have a great number of jobs here. Not everyone is suited for this work, but it allowed me to be provider for my family and a taxpayer. I was able to purchase a home and buy a car. To be an American—how people worldwide think what being America is all about. I think the Port of Houston is what America is to the world: a place to live, to work and to enjoy freedoms that are not experienced all over the world.

> I think the Port of Houston is what America is to the world: a place to live, to work and to enjoy freedoms that are not experienced all over the world.

As a third-generation longshoreman, I just looked at the fact that my dad was a hardworking, fair person. He had morals and my grandfather did as well. I think the Port allowed them and allowed my family to carry on that tradition of being honest people, fair working people, and being people that want to do the right thing. The Port allows a man to be a man in a real world in a real sense and be fair and honest and be a law-abiding citizen. I was taught that and I live it. I expect that out of my family as well. The Port means a lot to my family and I. ∎

Interview conducted by Rebecca Marvil on April 11, 2014.
Photo by Lou Vest.

TOM LIGHTSEY

The **DEEPER** *it is,* *the* **SLOWER** *you* **GO**

A MAJOR COMPONENT OF THE PORT'S MARITIME INFRASTRUC-TURE ARE THE HOUSTON PILOTS, WHO ARE RESPONSIBLE FOR NAVIGATING ALL OF THE SHIPS IN AND OUT OF ONE OF THE MOST DIFFICULT WATERWAYS IN THE WORLD. EVEN WHEN INSTRU-MENTATION AND TECHNOLOGY WERE RUDIMENTARY IN COMPAR-ISON TO TODAY'S EQUIPMENT AND COMMUNICATION DEVICES, SAFETY FEATURED PROMINENTLY IN THE PILOT'S DAILY WORK. THE HOUSTON SHIP CHANNEL PRESENTED ITS PILOTS WITH A TEST OF SKILL, SAVVY AND IN-THE-MOMENT CALCULATION UNPARALLELED ELSEWHERE. A MISTAKE COULD MEAN AN ACCIDENT; AN ACCIDENT, A DISASTER. CAPTAIN TOM LIGHTSEY SHARES SOME OF WHAT THE JOB WAS LIKE FOR PILOTS OF AN OLDER GENERATION.

Safety is a pilot's primary concern. Safety, safety, safety —that's what we get paid for, because one collision can be chaotic. The Channel is only four hundred feet wide. It's man-made. It's got steep banks, so the deeper it is, the slower you have to go because a ship will not get close to the bank because of the bank cushion. The closer you get to the side of the bank, the more the water going down the side will push the ship back out towards the center of the Channel. The media has called it "Texas Chicken" when two ships meet. You can't stop a ship, so you have to be very, very cautious.

The pilots know that you have to hold on when you are meeting head to head until you are about a half a mile apart. First-timer captains climb the wall because they think a collision is imminent, but it is not. We pilots have done it so much that we wait and then move just a few degrees over. If we get over too soon the bank is going to force you back into the center of the Channel. It makes all the people on the ship who haven't been here before really nervous. It is very dangerous. We had collisions before we had the good communication like we have now. We have had a pilot that has been burned to death in a collision, so that is the reason we preach safety. Safety is the primary concern, and we live and breathe safety.

I don't think it is as bad now, but they used to say that Houston was one of the most difficult and dangerous ship channels in the world. The company that I worked for [before I became a pilot] previously wouldn't load at night, because they considered it to be too dangerous. The ship would come in light, but we would not load it because of all those different chemicals we had. So, they were very safety-conscious [even then].

SHIP PILOT IS A DIFFERENT KIND OF OCCUPATION. THERE IS NO NINE-TO-FIVE WORK DAY BECAUSE SHIPS ARE COMING AND GO-ING IN THE CHANNEL AT ALL HOURS. IN THE PORT'S EARLY YEARS, THE REGIMEN WAS PUNISHING, DEMANDING COMPLETE CONCEN-TRATION WHILE ON THE JOB AND COMMITMENT TO A DAUNTING WORK SCHEDULE. ALSO, THE OLDER PILOTS, WHO LEARNED THEIR CRAFT BEFORE THE ADVENT OF CELL PHONES AND INSTANT ELECTRONIC COMMUNICATIONS, HAD TO REPORT TO A LARGELY UNKNOWN WORKPLACE—WHATEVER VESSEL WAS NEXT IN LINE.

When the phone rings for a dispatch, you don't know what kind of ship it's going to be, where it is going to be, or how deep it is. You may have to go to Galveston to bring it in or it may be up in the Turning Basin. You don't know if it is going to be loaded with grain or if it's going to be an eight-hour job. The good thing is, the pilots are on call for fifteen days, then off for fifteen days. During those fifteen days that you are on call you are either on the Channel or you are sleeping. It is a very good job for a working man.

Let's assume I'm on the pilot boat outside of Galveston, four miles outside of the jetties. The pilot boat goes alongside the ship. The pilot climbs a little small Jacob's ladder up to the main deck and then a crewmember escorts him up to the bridge. You introduce yourself to the captain and find out the particulars: the length, the breadth, the draft and the destination. Then, the pi-lot is in command. He makes all of the decisions, tell-ing the quartermaster what course to steer and telling

the mate where to put the engines. For example, tak-ing a big 150,000-ton loaded ship to one of the crude docks will probably take six hours, maybe even seven hours. The most difficult for me to learn was the integrat-ed tug and barges because I had come off of ships and these big sea-going tug and barges were a whole new ball game. It really wasn't that difficult, just required total concentration.

> *When the phone rings*
> *for a dispatch, you don't know*
> *what kind of ship it's going to be,*
> *where it is going to be,*
> *or how deep it is.*

HOUSTON PILOTS ARE A PROUD GROUP—SUPER COMPETITIVE AND STRINGENT IN TERMS OF THE LEVEL OF INDIVIDUAL SKILL AND CAPACITY EACH IS ACCOUNTABLE FOR, YET COOPERATIVE IN THE MANNER THEY ARE ORGANIZED. LIKE OTHER OCCUPATIONS ON THE SHIP CHANNEL, THEY HAVE MODERNIZED IN RECENT DECADES BY OPENING THEIR RANKS MORE FULLY TO COMMUNITIES THAT WERE NOT ORIGINALLY REPRESENTED IN THEIR MEMBERSHIP.

Every port has to have pilots. This makes it really good if you are one of the pilots—it is a good living. It is the top of the marine profession to be a pilot. I was a cap-tain but pilot is one step above that. The pilots own their own business. We have a commission from the state of Texas—the Port Commission is the Pilot Commission. The Port Commission sets our rates. We pool all the money, take the expenses out, and what is left we divide equally among the other pilots. There is no seniority system.

There have been so many improvements in my time since I started with the Houston Pilots. When I started, we had thirty pilots and we worked like dogs. We got off of one ship and there would be another one waiting for you. Now they work like gentlemen. We have taken minorities and we have taken women. It is a good job.

Right now when you finish a job, you are guaranteed twelve hours off. If you handle two ships you are guaranteed eighteen hours off.

ALONG WITH CHANGES IN MEMBERSHIP, SIGNIFICANT ENHANCEMENT IN COMMUNICATION TECHNOLOGY, AND EVER MORE SERIOUS ATTENTION TO SAFETY PROCEDURES AND PRECAUTIONS, THE JOB OF PILOTING NOW ATTRACTS MORE CANDIDATES WITH FORMAL MARITIME TRAINING. BUT IT IS WORTH NOTING THAT THE PROCESS OF QUALIFYING ALSO INVOLVES A MUCH LONGER APPRENTICESHIP PERIOD, POINTING TO THE IMPORTANCE OF THE KIND OF "LOCAL KNOWLEDGE" ONE CAN ACQUIRE ONLY FROM WORKING ON THE CHANNEL WITH PILOT MENTORS WHO KNOW THE CHANNEL FROM LONG, LONG EXPERIENCE.

It wasn't that way when I was there, but they have improved working conditions and now we have wonderful communications. Everybody has a laptop and they can pull it up and find out who the pilot is, how many tons the ship is and what the draft is. They can talk to each other. You had to be a lot more cautious back then. The safety has improved tremendously. Radar has increased and everybody is in constant contact. They know who they are meeting and overtaking. Today, everybody has his or her own VHF radios and cellphones. It has made all the difference in the world as far as safety is concerned.

Right now, you have to have a marine background to be a pilot. We take half "blue-water" men and half "brown-water" men, half steamship people and half towboat people. We found out that background doesn't make that much of a difference. It is a test of fortitude because you can get into some bad situations. It is a three-year apprentice program. When I came, it was only a year, but now they have moved it up. The new man has to ride with other pilots, then they gradually give him small ships or light drafts and then you progress. It is three years before you become a full pilot. But now, everybody has to have a maritime degree and come through one of those four-year colleges. I didn't have that. I was in the right place at the right time.

AND PILOTS ARE THE ULTIMATE FIRST RESPONDERS, NOT JUST MEETING THE SHIPS AS THEY COME INTO GALVESTON BAY, BUT GREETING THE WORLD AS IT ENTERS THE HOUSTON SHIP CHANNEL. PORTS ARE INTERNATIONAL ENTITIES, GATEWAYS TO THE GLOBAL ECONOMY AND AVENUES TO THE WORLDWIDE WORKFORCE. PILOTS TAKE THAT RESPONSIBILITY SERIOUSLY.

I have a little cheat book. I write down whatever I need to tell them in French, Spanish, Greek and Portuguese. I never got to Chinese. But I could talk directly to the quartermaster instead of to an interpreter. There is no room for error. When you talk to that quartermaster, you need to see where he has put that compass and where he has put the wheel and you are looking at the rudder indicator to make sure he is doing what you are telling him. If you can talk directly to him, in French, he likes that and everybody on the bridge likes that. I could do twenty words in five different languages and that made my job so much easier, but most of the pilots didn't do that.

> *I have a little cheat book.*
> *I write down whatever I need*
> *to tell them in French, Spanish,*
> *Greek and Portuguese.*

The big thing about the Port of Houston is we still have so much room to expand, and that's the key to progress. Houston has tripled in size since I came ashore. We didn't have Bayport, Barbours Cut or Ordinance Depot. They are constantly building new docks. I can't visualize what it is going to be twenty years from now. ■

Interview conducted by Pat Jasper on September 27, 2011.
©Houston Chronicle/Nick de la Torre. Used with permission.

Richard Bludworth holds a snapshot of his mother and father.
Photo by Loriana Espinel

[GENERATIONS]

IT IS NOT UNUSUAL FOR OCCUPATIONS TO BE PASSED DOWN from parent to child to grandchild. Businesses, in particular, tend to straddle generations. Children grow up in the midst of an enterprise, spending time informally absorbing the outlines of the venture or the nature of the trade. A founder may augment personnel at a new business by recruiting sons and daughters to assist. Young people in such families can spend summers and time after school helping with the more unskilled aspects of a business, such as staffing a counter or greeting customers or cleaning up the shop or grounds. Sometimes it is more obligatory than voluntary. Frequently, it is a tradition, just something that has always been a part of a family's history and identity.

On the Houston Ship Channel, any number of businesses were formed and continue to thrive over generations within families. For example, in 1935, Thomas Studdert, a man of sturdy Irish stock, founded Buffalo Marine. A bunkering company that is still vital today, Buffalo Marine is currently led by his son Patrick Studdert, who began working alongside his father in 1976. Nearly four decades later, Pat's son Tim plays a substantial role in the company's leadership. While Pat draws colorfully upon football metaphors to convey the importance of teamwork to his management model[1], it is the idea of family that informs the tight-knit network he builds among his employees through direct and personal interaction. This close identification of the corporation with the family is borne out tangibly in the names of some of the company's latest towboats, which have been christened with the names of Studdert family members, even those from the fourth-generation.

[1] Angela Liles. (2012, February 23). *Buffalo Marine Service, Inc.* [Video file].
Retrieved from http://www.youtube.com/watch?v=HAWHa9SSfqE

There was a time when this intergenerational family involvement in types of work along the Ship Channel was far more common than it is now. With open docks and ready access to many industrial areas lining the waterway, families could meet up at the worksite and actually see the places where their parents, mostly their fathers, worked and the kind of work they did. These experiences created an awareness—a vista of opportunity—for young people considering their future career possibilities. Sometimes, it led directly into a union or an occupation with which one's family was intensely identified—like becoming a boatman or a pilot. Sometimes, it suggested alternatives, but alternatives that were still identified with the Port and the Ship Channel. Often, the gritty and the backbreaking character of the work was the main motivation for young people to seek employment in a different sector than their forebears, or more education in order to find jobs that demanded less physical labor and offered more shelter from the elements. Even when newer generations moved away from the Port and Ship Channel as a possible profession, they tended to retain their loyalty to the place and the dignity of the family's work, whether blue collar or professional.

At the start of Steve Bennett's career, he could go directly down to the Channel to see how things worked; he spent much time there as a youngster. His mother would pile her children into the car to meet up with her husband as he came off his fifteen-day shift as a Houston Pilot. While Bennett ended up working on the Port, he went in a different direction than his father. He chose another profession to which he was almost habitually exposed in those early days. Every time they arrived to pick up his father, the elder Bennett would invariably be departing a boat that he had just docked. At the moment his dad's work was done, that of the lineman—who is responsible for securing the ships at dock—had just begun. Bennett recalls:

> When Mom would go to pick Dad up, she would always see these guys down there tying the ship up, and she'd always say, "Bob, you know, that's the job Steve needs to have. I know Steve would be good at that job." So, when I got older, Dad introduced me to somebody, a friend of his that was a boatman, which were the guys that tie the ships up. I started working part-time for the boatmen. This was in 1977, just as I got out of the Navy, so it would be about thirty-five years ago. I love this job. My job down here as a boatman has been great for me.

Bennett has since advanced; he is now ranked number five in seniority in the Houston Boatman's local. And, of course, he met his wife Crystal through his work. She too comes from a multi-generational family tradition of working on the Houston Ship Channel.

Joseph Kinch, on the other hand, followed directly in the footsteps of his forebears; he is a third-generation member of the International Longshoremen's Association (ILA). His grandfather, who came to Houston from Galveston in 1914 just as the Port was truly opening for business, co-founded one of the original Houston locals. His grandfather's story provides a fascinating context for the Port's history:

> My grandfather was born in 1876, the same year Custer got slaughtered at Little Bighorn. He left Louisiana about 1898 and moved to Galveston and started working on the waterfront. When the news came to Galveston that Houston was starting a port, him and Mundy Albright and Saul Ashford came up and established the International Longshoremen's union here. The group came and helped establish the 872 local in Houston. Once they did, the ships started coming in.

Kinch's father carried on the tradition. Joseph, however, initially sought an education at Southern University in Baton Rouge and then later at the University of Southern California. He studied to be an architect but quickly realized that there was better money to be had on the docks, especially for a young African American man with already well-established connections in the union. Like his father and grandfather before him, he became a part of the local leadership and served on the executive board of his local for many years. His family's history in the Houston ILA echoes all of the changes that the union has seen in the century-long life of the Houston Ship Channel.

The Tellepsen family has a storied connection to the Port spanning three full generations. Best represented on a day-to-day basis in this new century by Tom Tellepsen II, the family's involvement with the Ship Channel also dates back to the early part of the twentieth century. His grandfather, after whom he is named, followed his own father to the United States from Norway shortly after 1900. In 1906, he was convinced that the greatest opportunity for a young man was to be had in Panama, building the Canal. After a two-year stint in Central America, he settled in Texas and started a construction business that went on to build several of the important landmarks along the Ship Channel. His grandson and namesake describes several of them:

> *We are proud to have a family history at the Houston Ship Channel that dates back to 1922, when Granddad built the second dock of any consequence on the Channel called the Manchester Wharf. The following year, Anderson Clayton, one of the largest cotton merchants in the world, needed a dock at season's end. Granddad built this 1700-foot dock in a record ninety days using concrete piling, which was a first in Houston. That was the beginning of many projects over the years completed by Tellepsen on the Ship Channel. In 1949, they revamped the original Manchester Wharf and built the first docks at Barbours Cut in the 1970s under their heavy construction division.*

By then, the Tellepsen family's ties to the Port and Ship Channel had passed significantly into the second generation. Howard Tellepsen, Tom Tellepsen's only son, had joined his father in the business. In addition to being involved in developing the infrastructure of the Port, Tellepsen Builders was expanding their client base to the burgeoning petrochemical industries developing up and down the Ship Channel. His son Tom II recalls this period after his father had taken the reins of the corporation:

> *After World War II, Tellepsen expanded by adding a petrochem division, which once again led them to the Ship Channel. Their clients included oil companies who were, by then, entrenched on the Channel. I remember visiting one of their treatment plant projects for Shell Chemical in the late 1970s and dock construction for Phillips in 1980.*

In fact, his father had actually been appointed and served as Chair of the Port from 1956 to 1970. In 1970, at Howard Tellepsen's urging, the company made the commitment to begin construction of the International Seafarers' Center even before full funding for the project had been secured. It was named after him in 2006. Through the Seafarers' Center and numerous other

building projects, the Tellepsen's third- and fourth-generations have retained a strong relationship to the Port and Ship Channel.

A different kind of intergenerational family story connected to the Port of Houston is that of
Carlos de Aldecoa Bueno. A third-generation member of a coffee roasting and processing
company, de Aldecoa describes specifically why Houston and its port became a way to keep his
family tradition vital and thriving:

> *Our family business started in Spain, in Madrid, back in the 1920s. To-*
> *wards the end of the Spanish Civil War, they started a coffee roasting*
> *and packaging business in Mexico. My father opened a coffee roasting*
> *and packaging operation in the 1980s, just for the opportunity to look at*
> *different markets. He looked at the U.S. and he picked Houston because of*
> *the location of the Port, because for a commodity not grown in the U.S.,*
> *it had to be imported. Houston is strategically located mid-point between*
> *East and West coasts, so it is a central point for distribution. In the case*
> *of coffee, the Port is always going to be a huge component of that. And*
> *at the same time, we have benefited from the cost of natural gas and*
> *electricity.*

Like the longshoremen, some of the professions on the Ship Channel have a long history of fathers opening the doors for the sons or, at least, making access easier and connections inside the occupation more readily available. Much of that has changed over time. With the introduction of Equal Employment Opportunity legislation, discrimination on the basis of gender or ethnicity, or preference shown to workers' family members, has largely disappeared on the Ship Channel. Hiring practices have been regularized. Even the Boatmen's local on the Ship Channel had to reorganize their employment process in the 1980s to avoid nepotism.

Nonetheless, many families pride themselves on working in the same job over many generations. The Houston Pilots are no exception. But with obvious concerns about inappropriate preferences, the pilots have established rigorous guidelines, especially one that notes that family members may not serve together. Still, there are families in which the tradition is carried on (in the face of substantial testing and application procedures), and the Glass family is a great example why. Matthew Glass, whose father, Leonard, was a pilot for over twenty years, explains the allure:

> *Growing up in my house and seeing my dad do it, and seeing someone have such a passion and love for his job—how are you not going to love that? And not going to want to do that too one day? I mean it really is the world's coolest job. You know, I always grew up around the pilots: my dad and his friends. It's kind of a lifestyle. You work so closely together; you become so close. I mean, I've heard every sea story two or three times. So you grow up at these dinner tables hearing these sea stories and the butter knife becomes a ship, the salad plate becomes the dock. And now I find myself driving the butter knife across the dinner table explaining how the ship wouldn't stop or something interesting.* ▌

TOM TELLEPSEN

MARITIME ROOTS *and* BRANCHES: *One* FAMILY'S STORY

FOR SOME FAMILIES, MARITIME WORK HAS SPANNED A FEW GEN-ERATIONS. FOR THE TELLEPSEN FAMILY, IT HAS ALSO SPANNED CONTINENTS. HERE, TOM TELLEPSEN II TELLS HIS FAMILY STORY, FOCUSING ON THE WAYS IN WHICH THE PORT OF HOUSTON PRO-VIDED AN ENTRY POINT INTO DIFFERENT KINDS OF INDUSTRIES FOR THE FAMILY BUSINESS.

My grandfather was from Norway. He left his little town of Tvedestrand when he was fourteen years old. He worked as a cabin boy on a ship and for two years he circled the globe and worked on a sailing ship. I sup-pose the dream of every Scandinavian boy was to get to sea and eventually captain his own ship. Granddad had relatives in New York and when he was finished with his excursion, he landed in New York by way of Ellis Island. He sought work there and became a carpenter. Then he heard of a new and promising opportunity, which led him to the Panama Canal. He worked there for almost two years between 1906 and 1908. Granddad was en-couraged to go back to the U.S. to get his naturalization papers. He settled in Texas for a new start and started his construction career in 1909. In 1912, he sailed back to Norway and married his childhood sweetheart, Ingeborg, and brought her back to his adopted country. Their family grew with the birth of my dad, Howard T. Tellepsen, in 1913, followed by two sisters, Hortense and Lorraine.

> *I suppose the dream of every Scandinavian boy was to get to sea and eventually captain his own ship.*

In the meantime, Granddad started out as a one-man operation. He had an interest and a penchant for projects on the water, but he also liked heavy construction. He built the Miller Outdoor Theatre, the Museum of Fine Arts, one of the chemistry buildings over at Rice University, among others. We are proud to have a family history at the Houston Ship Channel that dates back to 1922, when Granddad built the second dock of any consequence on the Channel, called the Manchester Wharf. The following year, Anderson Clayton, one of the largest cotton merchants in the world, needed a dock at season's end. Granddad built this 1700-foot dock in a record ninety days using concrete piling, which was a first in Houston. That was the beginning of many projects over the years completed by Tellepsen on the Ship Channel. In 1949 they revamped the original Manchester Wharf and built the first docks at Barbours Cut in the 1970s under their heavy construction division. After World War II, Tellepsen expanded by adding a petrochem division, which once again led them to the Ship Channel. Their clients included oil companies who were, by then, entrenched on the Channel. I remember visiting one of their treatment plant projects for Shell Chemical in the late 1970s and dock construction for Phillips in 1980.

TELLEPSEN TELLS THE STORY OF HIS GRANDPARENTS' EARLY YEARS IN HOUSTON AND HOW THEY CAME TO BUILD A HOME FOR THEMSELVES IN THE EAST END. THE EASTWOOD SUBDIVISION WAS HOME TO MANY WHO INFLUENCED THE GROWTH OF DOWNTOWN AND THE PORT. BUT AS TELLEPSEN'S CAREER PROSPERED, HE DID NOT OVERLOOK THE ROLE OF WORKERS IN BUILDING THE CITY AND THE SHIP CHANNEL, AS HIS RELIGIOUS BELIEFS AND COMMITMENTS REVEAL.

My grandmother cried when they got off of the boat. My granddad had tried to explain that the terrain was somewhat flatter than the fjords of their native Norway but to no avail. Granddad vowed that they would eventually build a home for her that would be their little Norway. Their house was in the East End [1]. In 1923, while he sent his family to Norway for the whole summer he stayed behind to add a second story. The house has massive chains over the porch and a very substantial mast that came out of the wall of the second floor. It must have been twenty-five feet long and it draped over the porch and it always had the American flag on it. He built concrete ponds full of fish, a concrete bridge and a little waterfall. My family came back and they were very surprised.

My cousins and I would spend the night there and knew we had to go to his church. At the church, he commissioned an artist to build a mural behind the altar; it is still there today. He titled it "Christ of the Working Man." This tremendous faith in God also produced a faith in himself and his fellow man and a faith in liberty. He was so proud to be an American. It is a very unusual story of a Norwegian immigrant who didn't even know the language coming to Houston at a very young stage of his life to make his mark.

[1] The East End is a district just to the east of downtown Houston that includes two of the city's oldest neighborhoods: Magnolia Park and Second Ward. The East End was a primary area for attracting immigrants, including Germans, Italians and Mexican Americans that worked on or near the Port of Houston.

The family's sense of civic duty continued in the second-generation through the work of Howard Tellepsen, father of Howard Jr. and Tom II. Howard Sr. was also deeply involved in the Port of Houston Authority. Because of his civic engagement and role as a corporate leader, he could serve as a catalyst for projects that promoted both the profitability of the Port and the betterment of the workforce. This dual family legacy is a lasting one.

In 1956, my dad was asked to be the Chairman of the Port of Houston Authority. Following in his father's footsteps, he was able to branch out more and give of himself at a remarkably young age. He was forty-three years old when he was appointed as the Chairman, a role that spanned fourteen years until 1970. He was responsible for unprecedented growth with the help of a voter-approved bond issue. He was a rampant supporter of the Port of Houston because he realized its critical place in the economy of Houston. Many Houstonians have a vague understanding of this, but as my dad would say, it was always a challenge due to the Port's geographical isolation.

> This tremendous faith in God also produced a faith in himself and his fellow man and a faith in liberty. He was so proud to be an American.

IT IS FITTING, THEN, THAT THE CONTINUING LEGACY OF THE TELLEPSEN FAMILY GOES BACK, FULL CIRCLE, TO CARE FOR THE COMMON SEAFARING MAN. TOM'S FATHER WAS A CENTRAL FIGURE IN BRINGING THE SEAFARERS' CENTER INTO BEING, AND TOM AND HIS BROTHER CONTINUE TO SERVE AS STEWARDS FOR THE INSTITUTION TO THIS DAY.

Back in 1968, there was a semblance of a seafarers' center. They ran it out of a temporary building, but it was shabby. When Dad was Chair, some civic and Port leaders and chaplains got together, and in 1969 the Port leased nearly eight acres to the Seamen Center and the next big step was raising the money. There was such a need for the organization in the building at that time that my dad went to his dad and asked him for permission to start construction without the funding. Granddad agreed to that. In 1972, my dad was the MC of the opening of the center, and although he was not chairman anymore, he had such faith that people would give to it. The money was raised. Tellepsen built it. The first service was on Christmas Eve. There was a big soccer field where ship crews would play each other and a large swimming pool. In the mid-1980s, a pavilion with a basketball court was added. The Center was highly successful. My granddad, too, must have shared that same yearning for simple comforts as a seafarer over one hundred years ago. ▌

Interview conducted by Pat Jasper on March 29, 2012.
Photo by Loriana Espinel.

CARLOS *de* ALDECOA
BUENO

Going GREEN:
THE *Maximus* STORY

THE DE ALDECOA FAMILY STORY POINTS TO THE IMPORTANCE OF MULTIGENERATIONAL FAMILY BUSINESSES ASSOCIATED WITH THE PORT OF HOUSTON. IT ALSO HIGHLIGHTS THE WAY IN WHICH THE PORT AND SHIP CHANNEL'S ROLE IN GLOBAL EXCHANGE IS EXPRESSED IN THE INTERNATIONAL CHARACTER OF THE MANY BUSINESSES AND CORPORATIONS THAT RESIDE THERE. CARLOS DE ALDECOA BUENO BEGINS BY DETAILING THE ROOTS OF HIS FAMILY'S COFFEE BUSINESS.

Our family business started in Spain, in Madrid. My grandfather and my great uncle started it during the Spanish Civil War. There were a lot of issues with the availability of coffee, so they started a blend which is called Torrefacto. They would import the coffee from Central America and primarily roast it in Madrid for the Madrid market at that time. Towards the end of the Spanish Civil War, they started a coffee roasting and packaging business in Mexico, in Veracruz, in the city of Cordoba. [In colonial times] a large group of Spaniards went to Cordoba and started the city. Today, it is one of the strongest coffee growing regions in Mexico. It still operates today.

My father opened a coffee roasting and packaging operation in the 1980s, just for the opportunity to look at different markets. He looked at the U.S. as a growing opportunity. He was looking at a couple of different cities, and he picked Houston because of the location of the Port, because for a commodity not grown in the U.S., it had to be imported. Ultimately, Houston, even in the late 1980s, proved to be a great opportunity and a great move for my father. We were all born in Mexico, came here, started studying here, and went to high school and college and stayed in Houston—loved it ever since.

CARS, PETROCHEMICAL PRODUCTS, CONTAINERS OF GOODS—THESE ARE THE FORMS OF CONTEMPORARY CARGO WE ARE MOST ACCUSTOMED TO HEARING ABOUT. IMPORTER/EXPORTER DE ALDECOA GIVES US AN INSIGHT INTO ANOTHER MAJOR INDUSTRY THAT DEPENDS ON SOME OF THE NEW STRENGTHS OF THE PORT OF HOUSTON, ALONG WITH ITS WELL-SITUATED GEOGRAPHY AND READILY AVAILABLE ENERGY RESOURCES.

> *Our family business started in Spain, in Madrid. My grandfather and my great uncle started it during the Spanish Civil War.*

Houston is strategically located mid-point between east and west coasts, so it is a central point for distribution. The Port is extremely important if you are importing a raw material or even working from an export standpoint, as far as assembly and re-exporting. Houston is ideally situated. In the case of coffee, the Port is always going to be a huge component of that. The Port has had significant growth and has been a huge support for our industry and at the same time we have benefited from the cost of natural gas and electricity. The utility cost in a conversion process—making green coffee into roasted or decaf or a soluble—uses a lot of energy. The fact that we sit in Texas on a central interstate pipeline gives us the benefit of being very competitive on the global scale.

DE ALDECOA GUIDES US THROUGH THE OPERATIONS OF THE FAMILY COFFEE BUSINESS, ORIGINALLY MAXIMUS COFFEE, BUT NOW RENAMED ATLANTIC COFFEE SOLUTIONS, AND OWNED BY A CONSORTIUM OF WHICH HIS FAMILY IS STILL A PART. UNDER THE STEWARDSHIP OF MAXIMUS, THE COMPANY HAS DEVELOPED NATURAL AND INNOVATIVE APPROACHES TO COFFEE PROCESSING. HE ALSO DESCRIBES THE RELATIONSHIP OF THE COMPANY'S OUTPUT TO THE MAJOR BRANDS THAT WE RECOGNIZE ON OUR STORE SHELVES.

Typically a coffee bean is going to come in through the Port of Houston. We get coffee from twenty different countries. Coffee is grown across the world in the equatorial belt between the two tropics. Coffee will come into the Port of Houston and it will come in containers in 130 to 150-pound burlap bags. It will have to be moved from the Port terminals over to the warehouse operation where coffee will be put into storage, sample tested and brought here for processing.

According to the customer's specifications, we will bring the coffee in, put it in our silos and process it. So, this is the largest and most integrated coffee manufacturing plant in the Americas, because typically there is only a roasting operation, or an instant coffee operation, or a decaf operation. Here, we do everything you can to coffee. We roast it and pack it for food service or retail.

We can decaffeinate the coffee using a chemical-free CO_2 extraction, which is the future of decaffeination. Most of the decaf consumed today is processed with chemicals. So [our method] is a very advanced method that is good for the consumer and the environment. We also make instant coffee, which we brew at high pressures and high temperatures and extract it. It is a one hundred percent natural, pure form of converting green coffee into instant coffee. You can buy a jar of instant coffee or it can also be used for a flavoring. When you buy a Häagen-Dazs ice cream or you buy a Frappuccino, ultimately what they are using is instant coffee as a natural flavoring in the product. With coffee, there is no artificial coffee flavor because coffee is one of the more difficult components to replicate.

> *Houston is strategically located mid-point between east and west coasts, so it is a central point for distribution.*

Maximus Coffee is a really a large business-to-business relationship with strategic clients. Our business is tailored around servicing larger accounts—Maxwell House, Nestlé, Folgers and Starbucks. We are the only instant coffee plant in the U.S. We are also the largest decaffeination plant in the Americas, the second largest in the world. Companies will provide their own formula and we will do the conversion of their own coffee, or we will source the grain and give them a finished case product.

We move over a million pounds of coffee on a daily basis, so it is a high volume facility with very high standards of quality and safety.

DESPITE THE MANY BENEFITS THAT THE PORT OF HOUSTON HAD TO OFFER, THERE WAS A DOWNSIDE. DE ALDECOA DESCRIBES HOW LEADERS OF THE LOCAL COFFEE ROASTING INDUSTRY BANDED TOGETHER WITH THE PORT TO OVERCOME CERTAIN OUTMODED TAXING PRACTICES AND ENHANCE THE ENTIRE ECONOMIC LANDSCAPE.

Texas did not have the best port of entry for coffee—and that had to do with the ad valorem taxes. It was a tax to be paid on all commodities that had inventories stored in Texas at the end of the year. We had to really lobby because we were competing with European ports and we were competing with New Orleans, Miami, New York for making Houston a certified exchange port for the trade. That was a huge hurdle—to build market acceptance towards the Port of Houston being a coffee port, instead of just a chemical port, as the industry looked at it. So, jointly with the Port of Houston, we formed the Greater Houston Coffee Association, which is still alive today. We called the major roasters, we lobbied and we put a business case together. It is a great idea for private industry and the public sector to get together for a purpose that is good for the community, at the end of the day.

We put an economic model that showed the benefit of the removal of the ad valorem tax. When you look at it today, the Port has won, the industry has won and Houston has won. We have four to five different coffee warehousing operations as opposed to just one. There are a number of roasters here in Houston. There are a number of coffee trade houses that have opened, which lends itself to transportation businesses and warehousing operations and insurance industries. So, we have seen Houston go from being number five in the U.S., to being close to number one in the storage of green coffee. That is a huge victory that came with the support from the Port of Houston.

[*We move over a million pounds of coffee on a daily basis, so it is a high volume facility with very high standards of quality and safety.*]

The Port of Houston has really been a great advocate of our industry. We built the stage for global recognition of the Port of Houston as a friendly business port. In the food world, it wasn't really recognized, so I think setting the stage and getting the ad valorem exemption on green coffee really allowed us to continue to push and promote the Port of Houston. I think it benefits the Port and it benefits everybody involved in the whole supply chain. ∎

Interview conducted by Rebecca Marvil on April 15, 2014.
Photo by RODOCLIX.

RICHARD
BLUDWORTH

THEY *Built* BOATS,
They BUILT *Barges*

THE WORLD OF WORK IN THE HOUSTON SHIP CHANNEL IS BOTH LARGE AND SMALL. SCALE CAN OFTEN BE BREATHTAKING AND THE CHALLENGES OF WORKING IN THAT SETTING IMMENSE, YET MANY OF THE PEOPLE WHO HAVE WORKED THERE FOR YEARS, FOR GENERATIONS, KNOW EACH OTHER OR AT LEAST OF EACH OTHER. CERTAIN NAMES ARE ASSOCIATED WITH CERTAIN TRADES OR MARITIME LEGACIES. A GOOD EXAMPLE IS THE LONG LINE OF BLUDWORTH SHIP BUILDERS WHO HAVE MADE THE GULF COAST THEIR HOME.

Well, the best we can gather, the family came over from England sometime in the early 1800s, and sometime in the late 1800s moved across the country into Louisiana and eventually ended up in Rockport, Texas. At the time, they settled out on an island, just off of Rockport, which was eventually named Bludworth Island—and is still named Bludworth Island. It's adjacent to the shipping waterway.

They were raising children, fishing, probably doing some mechanic work, maybe building a few boats. They raised seven or eight children on that island in the vicinity of Rockport. Those children moved up to the Houston, Galveston, Port Arthur, Orange area of Texas. Most of them stayed involved in boat building and/or boat operations, probably up through my current generation. Some of us are still involved in the same businesses.

My grandfather was in the shipyard business working for other people in Galveston. He actually owned his own shipyard in Brownsville. And during the Depression he lost it.

SHIPBUILDING IN THE HOUSTON AREA HAS GENERALLY BEEN ASSOCIATED WITH SMALLER CRAFT—TUGS, BARGES, TOW BOATS — THAT ARE EASIER TO BUILD IN YARDS CONSTRAINED BY THE LIMITED REAL ESTATE OF THE SHIP CHANNEL. THESE ARE ALSO THE CRAFT THAT ARE IN GREATEST DEMAND IN THE AREA, SINCE THE CHANNEL NECESSITATES THEIR USE TO GUIDE LARGER VESSELS.

I was born in Houston in 1948 at St. Joseph Hospital, where most people in Houston were born at that time. My dad and my uncle were involved in the shipping business. They owned and operated tugs and barges. They started in business after the World War II, built their own boat, put it in service, and continued to build boats and barges up through the 1990s, at which time they went out of business.

When he got out of the service, he and his brother built a boat from a landing craft that they purchased with their savings and built it in my grandmother's yard here in Houston, launched it into the Houston Ship Channel, and eventually started their own business from it, from that single boat. They built a tugboat out of it: added decks and houses, additional engines, and basically turned that hull into a boat that they could push barges with.

They built boats for themselves and they operated boats. They built barges for themselves and they operated those barges. They built a connection system for barges that we're still building today. And, it's one of the three or four connecting systems in the world. And we are still building it today.

They had three to four ocean tugs and ocean barges that transported mostly bulk liquids in the U.S. and in foreign trade. They had boats traveling all the way down to South America, Africa, Europe, and also boats that traded within the continental U.S.

> They built boats for themselves
> and they operated boats.
> They built barges for themselves
> and they operated those barges.

SHIPBUILDING AND ITS OFFSHOOTS, THEN, WERE A NECESSARY ELEMENT OF BLUDWORTH'S UPBRINGING.

Actually, I grew up in an era where you were able to just about tag along anywhere. They worked for Dow Chemical. And I can remember being in Dow Chemical offices when I was very young. Every time they had boats out of the water getting worked on I was there. Sometimes during the summers I worked there for the business: pipe fitting, welding, deck handing, working in the engine room, any number of jobs—really summer after summer. I actually started working on the boats, riding on them at about 14.

HIS FATHER'S BUSINESS WAS BUT ONE AMONG SEVERAL BLUDWORTH FAMILY ENTERPRISES THAT INVOLVED SHIPBUILDING AND REPAIR. THE TRADITION EXTENDED WIDELY TO HIS MANY SIBLINGS.

He had three or four brothers and a cousin that started Bludworth Shipyard on Brady Island after the war.

And they did build quite a number of boats there. They were in business from about the same time period up through the late '70s, early '80s before they sold out. And when they sold out, a few of them spun off and started other yards, other places. And some of their sons started other yards. So there are a lot of related people that own unrelated businesses, or at least they did in the past. You actually had the Bludworths and the Bonds. And Lennie Bond is my grandmother's nephew. So he was actually a double cousin. And his son actually works for me. Actually, his grandson works for me.

> *... a few of them spun off and started other yards, other places. And some of their sons started other yards. So there are a lot of related people that own unrelated businesses, ...*

THERE WAS COMPETITION, ESPECIALLY AS OIL BUSTS AND COR-PORATE CONSOLIDATION TOOK THEIR TOLL ON SMALLER, MORE FAMILY-BASED SHIPBUILDING ENTERPRISES.

I would say they were all very friendly competitors. And most of the shipyards are still friendly competitors. I think we all have the same customers. Each one of us knows we're never going to get all the work. And while we may not be happy to share it, we are realistic enough to share the business, because everybody wants some competition to keep them honest. ∎

Interview conducted by Pat Jasper on January 6, 2012.
Photo by Loriana Espinel.

So Throw the Heaving Line Already.
Photo by Lou Vest

[KNOW-HOW]

AT THE PORT OF HOUSTON AND ALONG THE HOUSTON SHIP CHANNEL, for all of their one hundred years, knowing how to get the job done—whatever the job—has always been the priority. Unloading that cargo, captaining that tugboat, dredging that channel are all means to an end. The end is the dispatch and delivery of goods. The means is knowledge and skill. Over time, the knowledge and skills associated with the many jobs that make up a working port have changed with the modernization and diversification of the workplace.

The nature of knowledge is complex: it is, on the one hand, information, facts and data; on the other, awareness, experience, understanding and appreciation. And the acquisition of knowledge is equally multifaceted. One can accumulate knowledge through observation, participation, mentoring; another way is through books, study, formal schooling. All of these forms of knowledge and ways of garnering it constitute a kind of training for undertaking the task at hand. They inform a single action and then, that action, in real time, informs understanding of similar such actions in the future.

In other words, there is a difference separating informal learning and local knowledge from the kinds of knowledge an individual acquires in officially sanctioned settings like the classroom or at a computer terminal or interactive simulator. Despite change and modernization, work along the Houston Ship Channel has always relied heavily on local knowledge and traditional learning—whether it involved the right way to lift a sack or swing rigging, or how to pilot the Channel or place a container.

Of course, before containerization came to dominate the shipping industry, all goods were treated as piecework of some kind. Older members of the International Longshoremen's Association (ILA) describe the elaborate and, for the time, efficient ways in which they moved cargo. Each gang of eight longshoremen was divided up to perform different tasks and these tasks would rotate among the team members over the course of a job. This way a gang shared the work equally, all workers taking turns to spare their fellows from the most demanding tasks for a certain time span. The gang boss was the individual with the greatest seniority and hence longest experience and deepest understanding of the work. He would keep the work moving at an appropriate pace and mentor the newer workers in safer and easier ways to accomplish arduous tasks. As third generation ILA member Joseph Kinch recounts:

> We had to learn these things—learn what to wear in the hold. If you wore a t-shirt, you were not going to last long; you were going to burn out. If you get you a sweatshirt, and sweat and get that sweatshirt wet, then you were all right. You could make that summer with that sweatshirt. But it was a learning process of things that were small and common to people that were older because they had to work in the heat, so they knew, and they would teach you, and if you paid attention to them, you could make a day.

With containerization, dock work shifted, as ILA leader Benny Holland notes, from "a hot body" to the skilled manipulation of cranes and forklifts. Moving the enormous containers demanded complex machinery that must be driven and controlled. This new kind of work called for additional training and knowledge. But anyone who has ever learned to drive a car or bake a cake knows there is more to it than following written instructions, sitting in a simulator or reading a recipe. Local knowledge plays a part here because more experienced workers still share their understandings and mastery with younger workers in any number of occupations along the Ship Channel.

Environment and context also play a very substantial part in the application of local knowledge, especially with the introduction of complex machinery and certain forms of automation, because the setting in which work unfolds can greatly impact how it is conducted. A crane is only as good as its operator, and its operator is only as good as his or her training *and* experience working in uncertain weather, or on cramped docks, to move cargo of various dimensions. A worker can learn all about these variables in school, but nothing replaces the application of new information gathered through interactions with co-workers and the accumulation of long experience.

While containerization has driven massive change on the Ship Channel, steady advances in the engineering of equipment and vessels have also altered the work of many. Port engineers, for one, while always essential to the workforce, have seen the demands on their expertise expand exponentially. In the early days, a port engineer was a mechanic whose responsibility was the maintenance of a boat so that it remained a functional part of the fleet. The engineer was concerned with keeping engines tuned, replacing parts and general repair. To do their job well, engineers needed to be resourceful and able to solve problems as they arose in the course of work. Nowadays, many port engineers enter the field with a college background, but limited on-the-job experience. Houston Port Engineer Terry Thibodeaux notes how these two different knowledge sets complement each other:

I never had a lot of schooling or education. I just worked so many hours and learned it. But say there is a guy sitting right next to me who did go to college and learned all of it and we work really well together because he knows a different part of the work than I do. I need a lot of information from him and he gets a lot of information from me too. The person with a lot of hands-on experience knows how to troubleshoot or pinpoint exactly what needs to be done. The guy with all the education can help you out with the different products that you put on barges and the tonnage you can load on a barge.

And both kinds of knowledge and familiarity with the mechanical functioning of the vessels make engineers an important part of the boat and ship building process because these workers bring their experience to design and build-out. Boatbuilding was also a hands-on way for engineers to learn about a vessel's electrical, cooling and storage systems and the placement of fuel and oil tanks. This knowledge began to shift significantly as boats and ships transitioned from strictly mechanical and electrical entities to ones outfitted with more and more electronically controlled equipment. Yet, as Thibodeaux remarks, many of these innovations were launched by companies that did not themselves comprehend all the operational ramifications. Engineers and others were learning to run, calibrate and repair them at the same time that the companies that created them. Still, Thibodeaux stresses, his colleagues with educational training bring skills that broaden their mutual understanding of an incident or a vessel's capacity. Working together they can suss out effective solutions that address a problem in the moment or over the long run. Invariably, Thibodeaux notes, they learn from each other.

Maybe the best example of how local knowledge functions in relation to the Port of Houston is the diversity of skills a Houston Pilot must possess to negotiate the Ship Channel. Houston Pilots is the group that serves as guides to ships entering the Channel from all over the world,

working with the captains to bring their ships into and out of the Port. Originally, individuals invited to join the Houston Pilots were largely evaluated on their experience and long résumés serving as ship captains themselves. In the early days, it did not hurt to follow in the footsteps of a family member—usually a son emulating a father, especially because captains' sons were likely to have experienced steady exposure to a captain's work from childhood.

Captain Tom Lightsey, a retired Houston Pilot, has seen big changes in the work of the pilots over the nearly four decade span (1956 to 1993) of his career. During this period, reliance on mentors become even greater as larger ships and heavier traffic intensified the Ship Channel's navigational challenges

> *It is a three-year apprentice program. When I came, it was only a year, but now they have moved it up. The new man has to ride with other pilots, then they gradually give him small ships or light drafts and then you progress. It is three years before you become a full pilot.*

Lightsey makes a great case for why this level of local knowledge and the enormous reliance on experienced pilots is essential for the training of new ones. Houston's Ship Channel is so narrow that it presents incomparable challenges to the pilot:

> *The Channel is only four hundred feet wide. It's man-made. It's got steep banks, so the deeper it is, the slower you have to go because a ship will not get close to the bank because of the bank cushion. The closer you get to the side of the bank, the more the water going down the side will push the ship back out towards the center of the Channel. The media has called it "Texas Chicken" when two ships meet. You can't stop a ship, so you have to be very, very cautious.*

> *The pilots know that you have to hold on when you are meeting head to head until you are about a half a mile apart. First-timer captains climb the wall because they think a collision is imminent, but it is not. We pilots have done it so much that we wait and then move just a few degrees over. If we get over too soon the bank is going to force you back into the center of the Channel. It makes all the people on the ship who haven't been here before really nervous.*

Gordie Keenan provides perhaps the most compelling description for the nature of knowledge in his field. At this point in his career he devotes himself entirely to developing the skills and capacity of novice mariners. Because his job is to oversee training for Higman Marine Service, a tug and barge operator on the Houston Ship Channel, his understanding of the equation between local knowledge and technical expertise is finely tuned.

You can have all the electronics in the world, but to get around a bend with the current going in all different directions? And you have to make a bridge? They learn through experience and through each other. We have a lot of technology, but it still goes back to the basic skills that go back to the Mark Twain days: basically, understanding the rivers, understanding the canals, understanding how to line up a tow at a bridge. All these bridges are different depending on what the currents are doing, their flood and drought conditions. There is so much for these folks to learn and it is a lifelong process. A lot of the older guys will mentor. We do have computer-based training. We have seminars. But the fundamental training is peer-to-peer. These guys learn from each other as they go along. That is so important in this business. ▮

Today, workers use all kinds of tools to make their jobs easier.

Photos by Lou Vest

TERRY THIBODEAUX

FIXING EVERYTHING *from* TOILETS *to* BROKEN HEARTS

WHEN PORT ENGINEER TERRY THIBODEAUX FIRST STARTED WORKING IN THE INDUSTRY, THE EMPHASIS WAS ON BOAT MECHANICS AND MAKING SURE THAT THE VESSELS FOR WHICH YOU WERE RESPONSIBLE WERE IN GOOD RUNNING ORDER, ALWAYS AND IN ALL WAYS.

During my first twenty-five years on the job, I was all hands-on. Back then, as a port engineer, you had to do it all—mechanics, change pistons, liners, everything on the boat. You only took care of a certain amount of boats, so you had the time to go and do that. You learned how to troubleshoot problems. You learned how to work with the guys on the boat—how to get along with them and make everything work as a whole unit. You learned to fix every-thing—as I say—from a toilet to broken hearts. You fixed every single thing on the boat—whatever was broken.

BUT AS THE INDUSTRY CHANGED AND EXPANDED, THE PACE QUICK-ENED AND THE PORT ENGINEER'S JOB GREW INCREASINGLY SPECIAL-IZED. ENGINEERS BECAME ESSENTIAL TO THE DESIGN, DEVELOP-MENT AND OVERSIGHT OF NEW VESSELS AS THE THRIVING MARKET DEMANDED.

The industry has picked up tremendously compared to what it was used to. The waterways look like Interstate 10 as far as traffic and the equipment that is out there. The industry is getting so big it needs people to build [in advance of a contract] already knowing that they have a job for that equipment. For example, we hired a ship-yard to build us some boats and they built us three boats. It had a contract already. In other words, it already had a job. It wasn't just being built—it already had work. That is how most people are building their equipment.

Port engineers are there almost every day during the building of a ship. We watch and see how it is built and give a lot of input on where to put the fuel, the oil tanks, and how the ship is going to be loaded. The company that is building the ship might want certain safety issues installed, so we oversee that. The ship starts out as a sheet of steel. It is already drawn up in blueprints. They build the hull first, and then you stick whatever engines, gears and generators you want in it. The houses—the living quarters—are built on other departments of the shipyard. Every shipyard does it differently. They will weld them on and then they will put the wheelhouse on the top. The whole time that that is going on, as a port engineer, you are working with the electricians running the wires, the A/C people, the flooring people, everything on it. You are overseeing that job.

[
The waterways look like
Interstate 10 as far as traffic
and the equipment that is out there.
]

THIBODEAUX GAINED THIS DEEP-SEATED "KNOW-HOW" THROUGH EXTENSIVE YEARS OF EXPERIENCE. BUT AS THE ENGINEERING AND EQUIPMENT ON A BOAT MOVED FROM MECHANICAL TO ELECTRICAL TO ELECTRONIC, HE WORKED ALONGSIDE COLLEAGUES IN THE INDUSTRY TO ADAPT, HONE AND SHARE NEW KNOWLEDGE.

Back when I was turning wrenches, there were a lot of older engines and we kept them running as long as we could because downtime was not as bad, back then. You could hold a boat up a little bit longer in repair with some of the older engines. Now it's all electronic engines. There is a time frame involved too, and you have to get things done as fast as possible. Some of those older engines that I knew a whole lot about, they are still out there, but not nearly as many. So I learn as things move on. Everything has changed and you have got to change with it. For example, let's say Caterpillar or Detroit puts out a new style of electronic engine; they are pretty new at it too. Some-

times, they are learning [how to fix things] just as fast as I am. I am learning at the same time that the manufacturer is learning—as they are putting the equipment out there.

[
*I am learning at the same
time that the manufacturer is
learning—as they are putting
the equipment out there.*
]

Today, with a cell phone, you can take care of a lot more equipment. So when you take care of that much equipment, you have to contract a lot of that out. You might have one boat broken down in Florida, the other one is broken down in Baton Rouge and the other one is in New Orleans. So you are constantly hiring people in that area because you can't be all over the place like you used to be. If boats run over something and mess up the propellers, you find out what shipyard to bring it to.

RESOURCEFULNESS AND AN ABILITY TO LEARN FROM EVERY NEW SITUATION ARE CENTRAL TO THE JOB OF A PORT ENGINEER, BUT SO ARE RELATIONSHIPS WITH OTHERS IN AN INDUSTRY WHERE GOALS ARE SHARED EVEN WITH YOUR COMPETITION.

The marine business is really big but it is really small too, because we rely on everybody out there to give us a hand. Everybody knows each other very well because in this business a lot of people have lots of years in it. If you have that many years, you know every industry out there and all your competitors and you all work well together. You have to make it work. When you are at shipyards, you meet all the other customers that are there too. I might need some parts and another customer might have some, so I might borrow it and pay it back later. So, the marine business is real big but real small too.

THIBODEAUX IS KEENLY AWARE OF THE DIFFERENT KINDS OF KNOWLEDGE THAT NEED TO COME TOGETHER, BOTH IN EVERYDAY MARITIME WORK AND DURING EMERGENCIES.

I never had a lot of schooling or education. I just worked so many hours and learned it. But say there is a guy sitting right next to me who did go to college and learned all of it and we work really well together because he knows a different part of the work than I do. I need a lot of information from him and he gets a lot of information from me too. The person with a lot of hands-on experience knows how to troubleshoot or pinpoint exactly what needs to be done. The guy with all the education can help you out with the different products that you put on barges and the tonnage you can load on a barge.

> *The marine business is really big but it is really small too, because we rely on everybody out there to give us a hand.*

In one case, we had a collision between one of our boats and a barge. The boat punctured a hole in the barge. We needed to know what happened to the machinery that failed and caused this to happen. I let him know what happened to the engines, and he calculated how much water was going into a certain-sized hole to see whether this equipment would still float if it took on so much water. So my part on the boat and machinery side helped him a lot and his part let me know whether this unit was going to sink or float or what all we had to get started to help out there. They know that more than I know about that but when it comes to repairs, I know the repair side more than they do. So it really works out well. You need both kinds of people.

You have to keep safety up-to-date. Sometimes, you have quite a few emergencies and you really have to be on your toes. For example, you don't want the steering going out. Years ago, a boat's steering went out and it turned hard over. He had no choice and ran right into the rocks. Back then, we had single skin barges, today we have double hull barges. It was a single skin barge, so when it hit, it put a hole in the barge. We had to call all the people to come out and rope it off and try to save the oil in one certain spot. They even went out and stuck a mattress in to clog up the hole and slow it down until they could get another boat to it to pump the product out of that tank into another barge. You have the Coast Guard and a lot of people involved; it is very expensive. When you do have spills, you have to get people moving and hustling. You have to call all the right people to do those certain jobs. ▌

Interview conducted by Pat Jasper on November 14, 2010.
Photo by Lou Vest.

HOLLY
COOPER

I *am* THE PILOT. I *really* AM.

A CAREER AT SEA WAS UNTHINKABLE FOR WOMEN RIGHT UP INTO THE 1970S. IT WAS IN 1974 THAT THE STATE UNIVERSITY OF NEW YORK MARITIME COLLEGE AND THE CALIFORNIA MARITIME ACADEMY FIRST ADMITTED WOMEN CADETS. IN THE EARLY YEARS OF THE TWENTIETH CENTURY, A WOMAN WOULD HAVE TO DISGUISE HERSELF AS A MAN IF SHE WANTED TO SAIL. THE ONLY WAY FOR MOST WOMEN TO TAKE PART IN RUNNING A MERCHANT VESSEL BEFORE 1900 WAS THROUGH MARRIAGE OR BY BEING THE CAPTAIN'S DAUGHTER.

HOLLY COOPER IS A PIONEER IN HOUSTON'S MARITIME INDUSTRY. SHE WAS ONE OF THE FIRST WOMEN IN THE COUNTRY TO BE ACCEPTED INTO A PILOTS' ASSOCIATION. TODAY, SHE IS ONE OF ONLY FOUR WOMEN PILOTS IN HOUSTON. SHE RECALLS HER LOVE FOR SPENDING TIME ON THE WATER AND HOW SHE TURNED THAT INTO A CAREER.

I was raised with a father who had three daughters and no sons. He has always had a very open mind and believes that we can do anything we want. He saw this wayward daughter that was always running away doing sailing, scuba diving and surfing, and he said, "Oh gosh, we have got to get her into college." My father was working in Washington, D.C. for the Department of Transportation (DOT). During that time, in the 1970s, DOT oversaw the Maritime Administration, MARAD. I was going to go to the Naval Academy and decided that there was too much regimentation, so I went to Texas A&M in Galveston. When I came into the maritime academies, they had just opened up for women a few years before.

THE HOUSTON PILOTS ASSOCIATION HAS APPROXIMATELY A HUNDRED PILOTS, YET JUST FOUR OF THEM ARE WOMEN. HOLLY COOPER FACES CHALLENGES AT THE WORKPLACE DAILY; HERE SHE TALKS ABOUT HER LIFE AS A WOMAN IN AN INDUSTRY POPULATED MOSTLY BY MEN.

If you board down in Galveston, you have the pilot boat come alongside and you grab hold of the ladder, you climb up and the pilot boat takes off. This happened many, many times to me: I climbed on up and all of a sudden the pilot boat takes off and they go, "Oh, the pilot, the pilot! We need the pilot! Bring the pilot back." You have to tell them, "No, I am the pilot. I really am." There are times when I walk up to the bridge and they all just look at me and then they watch me intently for a while and then they finally start to relax.

I have been a pilot in the Houston Ship Channel for twenty years now. When I first came in I was trained by a lot of the old guys. I was kind of accepted as either a daughter or as a sister, which was nice. I was never the buddy—it was either the daughter or the sister—which is good because they trained me. I was accepted in this family.

> *He saw this wayward daughter that was always running away doing sailing, scuba diving and surfing, and he said, "Oh gosh, we have got to get her into college."*

If you look at how many women have a maritime background, the odds are that very few women have wanted to go to sea or have stuck it out. Family life has something to do with it. I postponed having a son until late in life. I was probably the first pregnant female as a pilot out here—I worked through seven-and-a-half months. It's funny because most of my fellow pilots didn't know I was pregnant. They just thought I was putting on weight.

BEING ONE OF THE FIRST FEW WOMEN PILOTS COMES WITH ITS SHARE OF HARDSHIPS, BUT HOLLY COOPER SAYS THERE ARE A NUMBER OF REASONS SHE LOVES HER JOB AND THAT HAS HELPED HER IN THE COURSE OF HER TWENTY-YEAR CAREER. HERE SHE TALKS ABOUT A TYPICAL DAY ON OPEN WATER FOR A PILOT TAKING A SHIP OUT AND BRINGING A SHIP BACK IN.

You have to know it very well, but you learn every day. I will never stop learning out here. I think the reason why I love this job so much after twenty years is because it's always changing. I don't know what I'm going to get next. I don't know what the Channel is going to be like or the weather or the crew on board. That's the intrigue for me.

Our schedule for the most part is two weeks on and two weeks off, a fourteen-day rotation. When you're on call you're literally that—you're on call 24/7. If you have two ships, you are required by law to have twelve hours off. Sometimes you have twenty, depending on the number of ships in and out that day. If you have one job you have eight hours off, sometimes twelve—it depends on how busy the day is. You go into the bottom of the list for rotation after a double. At any time we have about forty-five pilots on call usually, and we try to keep the numbers at that because it does get busy out in the Channel.

Usually if you're sailing there's two ways you can get a call. One is sailing: then you're given a two-hour notice. The phone rings. You get up, you take a shower, you get in your car and you drive over there. You board whatever dock you're assigned to. You board that particular ship. You go up the gangway. They help you with your bags hopefully. You're met by one of the able-bodied seamen. He escorts you to the bridge. You get up to the bridge; you set up your equipment. You make sure you check your traffic; you check in with VTS— Vessel Traffic Service. Then you talk to the captain, have a master pilot conference card—you hand him one— make sure everything is in working order. You take his word for everything. You know what your draft is—you can read it. You also know what your air draft is—that's something given to you. We have no way of surveying the ship. We just have the data in front of us. There's a pilot card that will tell the year built, the length and beam, the draft, the whole nine yards, and what flag she is. Once we get all that established the protocol is taken care of. We checked in with VTS—they tell us what the traffic is inbound and outbound. Then we're ready to roll. You have tugboats normally or you have a bow thruster and a tug. And you take in your lines. You have line handlers that let go the lines on the docks. You also have tugs that are tied up to the ship that assist pushing the ship in while you untie. You look at the weather—you look at just about everything imaginable before you sail. Once you get everything in, then you go ahead and give your dead slow ahead and slow ahead and get her moving southbound.

It is the captain's ship. Legally he is still responsible for that vessel whether he has a pilot on board or not. He can override a pilot, but we are hired for our local knowledge and most pilots—all pilots in Houston—have that experience. So we're relied on for that. We also know the traffic. We also know the handling characteristics of other vessels and of your tugboats. We know the protocol. The captain—he pretty much takes it from sea buoy to sea buoy. He's the one who navigates across the ocean.

BRINGING A SHIP BACK IN REQUIRES A SLIGHTLY DIFFERENT PROCEDURE.

You're given a three-hour call out. And you head down to Galveston. There you board a pilot boat. We have four in Houston. We have the Bayou City, the Houston, the Lone Star and the Yellow Rose—all Texas names. And they board you—we have a boat that will take us out to the big boat, which is on station 24/7. And we board that boat from the little boat and then we board on the ship. When you board a vessel inbound usually you do ten knots. So both the pilot boat and the ship are going ten knots. There is a pilot ladder that you climb aboard and that can be anywhere between ten feet or if it's a very laden tanker it can be three feet on up to thirty feet. So you need to pull yourself up that ladder. Sometimes

there is a companionway that will help you alongside with the ladder. So it's a very physically demanding job with upper arm strength. And not only that: when you get to the deck you have to climb many flights of stairs to get up to the bridge. And then you have your protocol with master pilot conference and the whole bit and then you steam inbound.

EVEN AFTER WORKING AS A PILOT FOR TWO DECADES, HOLLY COOPER SAYS THERE ARE STILL THINGS THAT SHE CAN'T GET USED TO. SOME THINGS WILL REMAIN DIFFICULT.

> *I was kind of accepted as either a daughter or as a sister, which was nice. I was never the buddy— it was either the daughter or the sister—which is good because they trained me. I was accepted in this family.*

One thing that does get you is that your Circadian rhythm is pretty much shot because you're on nights sometimes and days sometimes, and you don't know what your schedule will be and you have to sleep when you can.

[The most difficult things are] boarding the ladders and the hours involved—both of those. The hours are all over the place. You sleep when you can. Boarding the ladders, you really have to trust that that ladder is tied up properly up there. I've had it, and all of us have had it, where it slipped on us. You board in the rain. You board in freezing weather. And you just hope, because you don't know, that that ladder is secured at the top. That it's not going to pay out when you put your weight on it. So that's the most dangerous part of it. ∎

Interview conducted by Rebecca Marvil on May 19, 2014.
Photo by Loriana Espinel.

CAPTAIN
HARJIT SINGH
BAINS

LIGHTERING the LOAD

CAPTAIN HARJIT SINGH BAINS IS A MEMBER OF HOUSTON'S GROWING INTERNATIONAL COMMUNITY THAT HAS SUCCESSFULLY MANAGED TO CRAFT A LIVING FOR THEMSELVES IN THE SHIPPING COMMUNITY. THE FAST GROWING CHANNEL PROVIDES IMMIGRANTS WITH NUMEROUS JOB OPPORTUNITIES. A MICROCOSM OF THE CITY ITSELF—THE HOUSTON SHIP CHANNEL IS A PLACE WHERE PEOPLE FROM MANY BACKGROUNDS CALL THEIR WORKPLACE.

Punjab is landlocked, so no one in my family had ever been out to sea. I was the first in my family to join the merchant navy in 1976. I completed my college education in Punjab, while my maritime education was on a training ship, T. S. Rajendra, at Bombay. Following the training, I obtained all of my maritime licenses from India. From 1986 to 1989, I was a Master (Captain on board merchant ships) in an Indian company called Great Eastern Shipping Co. It was one of the best shipping companies in India and renown around the world. After 1989, I joined Univan Ship management in Hong Kong. In 1995, I quit sailing and in 1996 came to the United States. First, I lived in the Bay Area of California, and then from California, my family and I moved to Houston, Texas. Houston had a lot of opportunities. Since 1997, I've been involved in different aspects of work in the shipping industry.

[
*Punjab is landlocked,
so no one in my family
had ever been out to sea.*
]

WHILE THE DEPTH OF THE HOUSTON SHIP CHANNEL TODAY IS FORTY-FIVE FEET, IT STILL RE-QUIRES REALLY LARGE VESSELS TO REDUCE THEIR DRAFT BY A PROCESS KNOWN AS *LIGHTERING* IN ORDER TO ENTER THE PORT FACILITIES. LIGHTERING IS SIMPLY SHIP-TO-SHIP TRANSFER OF OIL CARGO. BAINS WORKS AS A CONTRACT LIGHTERING ADVISOR WITH SEARIVER MARITIME INC. FOR AT-SEA LIGHTERING OF EXXONMOBIL CORPORATION

CARGOES AND EXPLAINS THE CAREFUL AND EXACTING PROCESS INVOLVED.

Lightering is used because economical shipment of crude oil from its source to the United States requires the use of extremely large tankers called very large crude carriers (VLCCs) and ultra large crude carriers (ULCCs). In turn, ports may not be deep enough, or have narrow entrances, or have small berths, such that these large tankers cannot be accommodated. Thus, lightering allows offshore unloading of the crude oil cargoes of the very largest tankers.

[
... lightering allows offshore unloading of the crude oil cargoes of the very largest tankers.
]

THE PROCESS OF LIGHTERING IS A BIG, BUT AT THE SAME TIME, DELICATE OPERATION. IT CAN BE DONE WHILE THE SHIPS ARE AT ANCHOR, DRIFTING, OR UNDERWAY. IT IS ALWAYS A JUDGMENT CALL, BASED ON THE CIRCUMSTANCES OF THE MOMENT AND ESPECIALLY THE VAGARIES OF THE WEATHER. BAINS EXPLAINS HOW AND WHY THIS MAKES A DIFFERENCE.

The lightering process consists of maneuvering a smaller tanker (service vessel) alongside the larger tanker or STBL (ship to be lightered), typically with both vessels underway. The two vessels are moored together. A portion of the crude oil cargo from the larger ship is discharged through hoses connected between the two vessels to the smaller ship.

The two vessels may be anchored or may continue underway while the transfer takes place, depending upon sea conditions. Lightering locations are dictated primarily by water depth and traffic. In the Gulf of Mexico, this process takes place twenty to sixty miles from land.

Under normal conditions, both vessels are under way at a pre-agreed speed until the vessels are safely moored together. The speed and course of the STBL, as well as the relative movement between the two vessels is periodically verified. As the STBL maintains her set course and slow speed, the lightering tanker maneuvers alongside. It slowly edges closer to the STBL until it matches course and speed. As the two vessels come near together, they are as close to parallel as possible, so that all four fenders simultaneously share the load of the impact. Mooring is done by the crew of each vessel involved in the operation. Upon completion of mooring operations, a qualified member from each vessel is stationed at the manifold during the entire transfer. During the cargo transfer, the STBL keeps a proper bridge watch to ensure that a safe anchor position is maintained; or if slow steaming, that safe navigation is carried out. The pumping of cargo commences at a slow rate, but when flow has been established, and no leaks found, the STBL increases pumping pressure to optimum rate of about 50,000 barrels per hour. All hose connections are continuously monitored for leaks.

When transfer is completed, hoses are drained, transferred to STBL (if more lighterings are due) or are returned to the service ship. The unberthing is carried out with the both vessels underway. The STBL is instructed by the merchant marine to maintain a speed and course previously agreed upon. During unmooring, plenty of slack is given on the mooring lines and good quality messenger lines are used to avoid difficulties in removing the eyes off bitts. One whole ship-to-ship operation, from the time the service vessel approaches the STBL to vessel castoff is completed in about eighteen hours. ▪

Interview conducted by Harold Dodd on March 23, 2013.
Photo by Jack Potts.

STEVE
BENNETT

I CALL *myself* A BOATMAN

STEVE

THERE ARE MANY JOBS ALONG THE SHIP CHANNEL. THE JOB OF A BOATMAN, OR LINE HANDLER, MAY AT FIRST GLANCE SEEM RELATIVELY STRAIGHTFORWARD, WHEN IN FACT THE TASK OF TYING AND ANCHORING A BOAT TO A DOCK IS DANGEROUS AND COMPLICATED WORK. STEVE BENNETT EXPLAINS.

I call myself a boatman, a line handler, but I use that term only when I'm filling out an application for something. That is when they don't know what a boatman is and then I put "line handler." The stickers on our trucks say "boatmen." We are the line handlers.

When we're called to tie the ship up at the Port of Houston, say at City Docks, Barbours Cut, or Bayport, we get down there before everybody else, and we'll tie the ship up, and as we're there, the other longshoremen and stevedores are showing up to unload the ship. So, we get there, we do our job and we're gone to another job. When they're through with unloading, and the ship's ready to sail, they call us, we come back in, we turn the ship loose and then we're gone again.

For example, my office will give me a call and say, "I have a job going to City Dock 30. He's inbound at Shell." I'd say, "Yes, I'm going to make it." I get up, get dressed, get in my truck, fight traffic, get down to the dock and wait for the ship. The ship comes alongside. I have my radio on, my handset, so that I can listen to the Port of Houston as they are spotting the ship. The Port of Houston police will spot the ship where they want the ship. The ship gets in position. We have usually two guys on each end of the ship—two on the bow and two on the stern. Guys on the ship will throw a heaving line over. It has a monkey fist on it. They throw it off the ship to the boatman on the dock. We'll pull the heaving line off the ship and put it on the bit. We have to take the heaving line off of that line and throw it back up to the ship. They tie another one on; we pull it over and put it on the bit. The spring line's first, then we put the stern lines out.

THE WORK OF A BOATMAN IS SOMETIMES ON A MASSIVE SCALE.

There are usually two men on each end when we're tying the ship up. Sometimes we have to use our trucks because the lines are so big, when there's a twenty-foot pull from the water up to the top. When these lines get wet, they soak up a lot of water. Sometimes the big giant ships we have coming in here that are 800 foot long are easier and faster to tie up than the little bitty, say, 400-foot ship because of the docks they go to and the kind of lines they have. It could take anywhere from fifteen minutes to tie up a ship to one-and-a-half hours. It depends on the situation, the dock, the ship and the crew on the ship. I like the fifteen-minute jobs better, but they're not all that way. There's only, say, seventy-five of us that

actually tie the ships up. It is all experience. That's one thing I got a lot of—knowledge—the older guys have a lot of knowledge. I mean the newer guys come on and want to start running boats and all, you know, they may run the boat good, but they hadn't seen a lot of the situations that I have.

In the olden days, you might be the only guy pulling them up. So you got one guy tying up one end of the ship, one guy tying up the other end of the ship, wiping your back out, your hands, whatever.

> [..., we get down there before everybody else, and we'll tie the ship up, and as we're there, the other longshoremen and stevedores are showing up to unload the ship.]

When it comes time to turn the ship loose, there'll be two of us coming down there. One would be on the stern; one would be on the bow. The ship will slack the head lines and the stern lines. We will throw them off, and then the ship slacks the spring lines, and we'll release the springs, and the ship goes on its way. That's your basic sailing.

When the ship goes into a chemical dock or a crude terminal, say the ship is 800-foot long, 136-foot wide, and probably has a draft of about forty, forty-two feet under the water. I'm in a boat now because all the lines had to be run by boat with the way the dock is set up. One guy is running the boat. Then there's one guy who stands behind the boat operator and wraps the lines off when we get them on the boat, and one guy decking, taking the lines on the forward end of our boat as they slack them down. The boat operator has to hold the boat steady, even though the wind and the water affect this. The deckhand will get the line on the bow, run it down on the port side of the boat. The swamper in the back of the boat has a small half-inch line that he uses to secure the ship's line. Then, the boat will take that line over to the hook and put it in the hook, and then we release that line. They heave that line up and then we go back and do it again on the next line. If I'm running the boat, I'm squatting down like a Major League catcher in the baseball game. My knees are shot now after doing this for thirty-five years.

[
If I'm running the boat, I'm squatting down like a Major League catcher in the baseball game. My knees are shot now after doing this for thirty-five years.
]

BENNETT'S APPRECIATION FOR THE KNOWLEDGE OF OLDER WORKERS PERHAPS RESIDES IN THE FACT THAT HE IS SECOND GENERATION ON THE WATERFRONT. AS THE SON OF A HOUSTON PILOT, BENNETT WAS EXPOSED EARLY TO WORK ON AND AROUND BOATS AND SHIPS. IT PROVIDED AN ENTRÉE INTO HIS CAREER PATH FOR HIM AND THAT OF OTHER FAMILY MEMBERS.

When Dad would bring a ship in, he would call when he'd get close to the dock. Mom would load us all up in the station wagon to pick Dad up because as a pilot he worked fifteen days on, fifteen days off. Finally, after what seemed like an hour, Dad would come walking up the docks in his khakis and smelling like crude because of the ship he was on. Even to this day, when I smell that crude smell, I think of Dad. When Mom would go to pick Dad up, she would always see these guys down there tying the ship up, and she'd always say, "Bob, you know, that's the job Steve needs to have." I didn't know it, but she said, "I know Steve would be good at that job." So when I got older, Dad introduced me to somebody, a friend of his that was a boatman, which were the guys that tie the ships up. I started working part-time for the boatmen. This was in 1977, just as I got out of the Navy,

so it would be about thirty-five years ago. I love this job. My job down here as a boatman has been great for me.

My sister, she went to college in Galveston and got her third mate's license and she went on and worked out on a ship out in Portland, Oregon and Seattle also. She finally got her captain's license. My wife Crystal's brothers work on the Port and her nephew is working on the tugboats for Harbor Tugs here at the Port of Houston. It all started from a kid—my dad, seventeen and barefoot—walking with his cousin to go to join the marines during World War II. While hitchhiking, a chief petty officer in the Coast Guard picked them up and told him about the Merchant Marines. And that's where they went instead.

[
I love this job. My job down here as a boatman has been great for me.
]

I wish I could still take my kids down there to the Port to watch me do my job. You can go out there and watch the ships go by. You can even go out to Galveston right there at the end of the seawall, and watch all the ships anchored or coming up and going out. It's pretty cool, but it's not like being able to take the kids down to the docks, you know. I wish my son would have worked on the Port, but, you know, he's got his own life. But I got hope for my grandson. I think he's going to do it one of these days. He seems interested now. ▮

Interview conducted by Pat Jasper on January 12, 2012.
©Houston Chronicle/Nick de la Torre. Used with permission.

JAMES PATRICK
COONEY

The THINGS *that* *Admiralty* LAWYERS DO

ON ANY GIVEN DAY, HUNDREDS OF SHIPS ARE COMING AND GOING ALONG THE SHIP CHANNEL IN THE PORT OF HOUSTON. LONGSHOREMEN LOAD AND UNLOAD CARGO, AND CAPTAINS AND TUGBOAT OPERATORS WORK TO NAVIGATE SHIPS AND MANEUVER A SEAMLESS STREAM OF CONTAINERS AND VESSELS. IT IS SERIOUS AND OFTEN DANGEROUS BUSINESS. THERE IS NO BETTER WAY TO GET AN INSIGHT INTO THE RISKY SIDE OF THE PORT ENVIRONMENT THAN TO TALK TO ADMIRALTY LAWYERS. SO WE ASKED JAMES PATRICK COONEY TO TAKE US THROUGH HIS LINE OF WORK—MARITIME LAW.

The things that admiralty lawyers do run the gamut. The high mass, if you will, of the admiralty practice used to be collisions and the problems that ships have navigating, such as grounding, hitting docks, hitting bridges and the like. Now it is oil spills, pollution matters, environmental things that result from the traditional casualties. Admiralty lawyers also do a huge amount of personal injury work. If you are an American seafarer, you are protected by the Jones Act[1]. If you are a longshoreman, shipyard worker or other non-seaman maritime worker, there is the Longshore and Harbor Workers Compensation Act, which provides both for worker compensation benefits and negligence claims against ship owners and others. This extends to the offshore oil industry where many offshore workers are covered by maritime law.

[*The things that admiralty lawyers do run the gamut.*]

Admiralty lawyers also deal with more mundane issues, such as immigration issues, from simple stowaways on board, to crew visa status and even the expatriation of dead bodies. For instance, if somebody dies on a ship, lawyers may get involved handling the legal niceties to get the body back to wherever home is or was. Then, there is the whole world of cargo claims—dealing with damage or loss of everything from the steel that comes

[1] The Merchant Marine Act of 1920, also known as the Jones Act, requires that all goods transported by water between U.S. ports be carried on U.S.-flag ships, constructed in the United States, owned by U.S. citizens, and crewed by U.S. citizens and U.S. permanent residents.

into the port to containers, specialized project cargoes, automobiles, liquefied natural gas, chemicals and crude oil—virtually anything that can be carried by ship.

Handling casualty work in the maritime arena is so different than handling domestic insurance claims, where files are sent to the lawyer after the lawsuit has been filed. I have been on ships to conduct an investigation before the body has been removed or before the deck has been cleaned of blood and after a collision while the ships were still sticking into each other. The last major oil spill I was involved with happened at eleven o'clock in the morning and I was on the scene at two o'clock that afternoon. There is a rapid response function, a 24/7 response component to the business for those who enjoy that sort of thing.

COONEY NOTES AN INTERESTING HISTORICAL POINT: THAT THE INSURANCE BUSINESS EMERGED INFORMALLY FROM MARITIME COMMERCE. AS EARLY AS 1688, A COFFEEHOUSE NAMED LLOYDS WAS A SITE WHERE BUSINESSMEN BARTERED OVER SHIPPING. THE COFFEEHOUSE WENT ON TO BECOME THE WORLD'S BEST-KNOWN INSURER, AND THE INSURANCE BUSINESS DEVELOPED INTO AN INTEGRAL AND COMPLEX COMPONENT OF THE MARITIME INDUSTRY.

To understand the practice of maritime law and shipping in general is to understand the role of insurance. Insurance finds its origins in ocean shipping. Lloyds of London started out as a coffeehouse for people who were basically making wagers whether a ship full of tea was going to make its way back from India or China or not. It was sort of, "if it doesn't show up I will pay you X." This became more formalized, so the first kind of insurance policies were hull policies insuring the physical existence of the vessel or policies covering the loss or damage of the vessel's cargo. Then they started branching out and covering other things like collision, cargo and other liabilities, giving rise to protection and indemnity clubs, associations of ship owners who share their liability risks. Thus, on the casualty and risk side of the business, marine insurance, for the most part, pays the lawyers' freight.

COONEY'S STORY ABOUT A SINGLE INCIDENT ILLUMINATES THIS COMPLEXITY, ESPECIALLY WHEN ACCIDENTS INVOLVE INTERNATIONAL ACTORS, NUMEROUS BUSINESSES, GOVERNMENTAL AGENCIES, CREWMEMBERS AND LOCAL RESIDENTS.

Back in 1984, a U.K. tank vessel named Alvenus grounded off Cameron, Louisiana, while going into Lake Charles. The bow bent up to about a fifteen-degree angle and the ship's sides split open and out spilled ten thousand tons of crude oil. It was just that sudden. I was involved in the response and subsequent handling of the incident and I have always described it as a five or six-ring circus, with multiple acts playing out in different rings. The oil migrated down the coast and came ashore on Galveston, and it turned out to be the largest beach amenity spill in the United States.

> Lloyds of London started out as a coffeehouse for people who were basically making wagers whether a ship full of tea was going to make its way back from India or China or not.

It was absolutely fascinating—a British vessel, a Coast Guard investigation, an investigation by the British government, a salvage operation, a mystery illness on the ship and lots of entities either suing or being sued. By the second day, we had twenty-five attorneys working on that case doing just a little bit of everything. You have to remember, this was before the enactment of OPA 90[2]; the development of an organized spill response industry, and those involved in the response were basically making it up as we went along.

[2] Oil Pollution Act of 1990 (OPA 90) is the comprehensive federal law to mitigate and prevent civil liability from the future oil spills off the coast of the United States.

The British government sent over a master mariner to investigate. We had the Coast Guard investigation. We had a litigation cranking up and we were taking depositions. We were managing the spill. We had a salvage operation going on. On top of everything else, everybody on the ship was coming down with painful boils on their body and we couldn't figure out what was going on. So we finally got one of the affected crew members on a helicopter and flew him to John Sealy Hospital in Galveston, very quietly. The Coast Guard knew what we were doing, but this was done very quietly because we did not know what we had out there.

It turns out that it was an infection from the hair follicles from a type of moth that flew into the ship's air conditioning system, died and decomposed. With the right diagnosis, the malady was controlled. With that mystery solved, we went on to clean the beaches (which took over two months), handle the litigation and after an almost three-month trial some five years later, brought the matter to a conclusion. It was a fascinating time.

ANOTHER INCIDENT REVEALS THE PRECISION AND DETAILED COMMUNICATIONS REQUIRED TO MAKE A SUCCESSFUL NAVIGATION DOWN THE CHANNEL. IN SOME CASES, INTERNATIONAL FACTORS COME INTO PLAY VIA CULTURAL MISCOMMUNICATIONS THAT CAN HAVE DANGEROUS RAMIFICATIONS. IN THE EPISODE RECOUNTED HERE COONEY HYPOTHESIZES THAT ONE SIMPLE GESTURE, WITH DIFFERENT MEANINGS FOR DIFFERENT CULTURES, CAUSED A MAJOR ACCIDENT.

To bring the ships into the turning basin in the Port of Houston, you go under the 610 bridge, which has a clearance of 135 feet depending on the tide. You have to lower the ship's boom (a long beam projecting from the mast of a derrick to support or guide cargo). Late one evening in December, I get a call that a cargo ship has hit the bridge. It didn't just simply hit the bridge: the ship's boom was facing forward, caught underneath the structure, went vertical and through the pavement, up and then back down again. I think there were three au-

tomobiles involved. Nobody got hurt badly. The boom comes back down, bends down towards the ship in a configuration, so it is literally a spring.

I get out to the ship at about two o'clock in the morning. The Coast Guard is out there trying to figure out how he hit the bridge. The shipping line primarily used chartered vessels and Eastern European crews. This particular ship had Polish officers who were very competent guys. However, the management company had just begun using Filipino crews (also very competent) to serve under the Eastern European officers. As on most ships these days, the primary language used on the ship was English. During the course of my investigation, it became clear to me that there had been a classic misunderstanding based on subtle cultural differences, although nobody would quite own up to this.

Before a vessel goes under a bridge, one of its navigation officers—in this case the chief officer—does an air draft calculation. He checks and sees what the draft of the vessel is, and it tells him how high in the water the vessel is. He checks the tide and basically confirms that the ship can safely pass underneath the bridge. Before doing this calculation, the chief officer had told the boatswain to lower the boom to forty-three degrees, which would make the boom low enough to get under the bridge.

The chief spoke in Polish-accented English and the boatswain speaks in Filipino-accented English. When asked to lower the boom and when asked to confirm that the boom had been lowered, the boatswain did not fully understand what he was being told or asked. But, as any polite Filipino would do, he nodded to the chief, really trying to say that he really did not understand. The chief instead took the nod as confirmation that the boom had been lowered and proceeded. Procedures and practices are now in place to avoid such misunderstandings, but in the early days when ship managers were moving away from single nationality crews, unfortunate misunderstandings such as this could occur. In a way, it points to one of the aspects of maritime practice I find most interesting: the need to attune yourself to subtle differences in culture and language, even if everyone is speaking in English.

> ...one of the aspects of maritime practice I find most interesting: the need to attune yourself to subtle differences in culture and language, even if everyone is speaking in English.

IN A FINAL STORY, COONEY ILLUSTRATES THE WEB OF ECONOMIC, HEALTH-RELATED, ENVIRONMENTAL AND, MOST IMPORTANTLY, LEGAL FACTORS RELATED TO MARITIME LAW.

I have been to a lot of big spills. Our job as maritime attorneys representing the spilling vessel initially is to make sure the response is being handled responsibly and that all the legal and regulatory requirements are being met. Then as far as the response goes, it is our job to get out of the way and let the experts do their thing. Our focus then shifts to the handling of claims from those who have been affected by the spill. The oil involved in the Port Arthur spill in 2010 was high sulfur crude, which gives off a strong smell of rotten eggs. Because of the fumes from the spilled oil, a very small area immediately next to the docks in Port Arthur was evacuated. The sequence leading up to the collision that resulted in the spill was fairly complicated. As the ship was coming up the channel, it started having a hydrodynamic interaction with the channel bank on either side and it sheered to one side and then the other. It did this four times, essentially bouncing off the sides of the channel. On the final sheer, it hit a ship at the dock and while it was sitting there—not impaled but sitting up against the other ship—an outbound barge came in and literally knifed into it, cutting through the double hull and into the center tank,

which was full of crude oil. It was the biggest spill we have had in Texas since 1990.

By deep-water standards, it was a relatively small spill. Because of the fumes that spilled out, there was the possibility of personal injury claims due to the inhalation of the fumes. Such claims are not covered by pollution statutes, which cover economic damages, but not personal injury claims. We knew we were going to get some personal injury claims, so the vessel owner filed a limitation of liability in the federal court in Beaumont. In a limitation action, the federal judge has to issue all sorts of orders which we had to send to all known claimants. One order provided for a cost bond which is normally in the nominal amount of $500. However, the judge scratched out $500 and put $1000 in ink. This order was sent to the claimants, about 2500 residents, who had made complaints. Somehow, the $1000 notation on the cost bond was misinterpreted and, as we later were told, the word got around in Port Arthur that if a person filed a claim, he or she would automatically get $1000, no questions asked. So, all of a sudden, the clerk's office was being inundated with thousands of claims, some from people who were not even in Port Arthur when the spill happened. In the end something like forty percent of the population of Port Arthur filed a claim. As a result, the court is still sorting through who is really entitled to assert a claim in the limitation action. But for this, the response and clean up process for the 2010 spill was a model of efficiency, evidencing how far the spill response industry has come from the days of the Alvenus in 1984. ▮

Interview conducted by Pat Jasper on February 24, 2012.
Photo by Lou Vest.

Detail: *History of the International Longshoremen's Local 872* by John Biggers.
Courtesy of ILA Local, 24. Photo: Neiman Catley.

[STRUGGLES]

CHANGE IS A CONSTANT AND IT IS A STANDARD PART OF ANY WORKPLACE. Locations change; employees leave, new ones come on, others advance; demand for certain goods waxes and wanes; equipment, machinery and technology continue to evolve; job qualifications, certifications and credentials are constantly modified and adjusted; legislation is enacted and amended; economies fluctuate with the good times and the bad. And in a workplace as complex as the Houston Ship Channel, each of these issues plays out differently across the diverse trades that are plied there.

Change can disrupt and disruption means struggle—struggle to oppose, to alter, to adapt, to adjust, to thrive, to succeed. Even before the Port of Houston was christened by city, state and federal authorities in 1914, the struggle to bring an imagined port into actual being was underway. The *primary* struggle of these early days was the effort of creation: to build, from the bottom up, a deep waterway directly into the city. Fully man-made and maintained through arduous labor and ingenious planning, the Port of Houston and its Ship Channel were dredged and excavated from the bayous and riverbeds of the region.

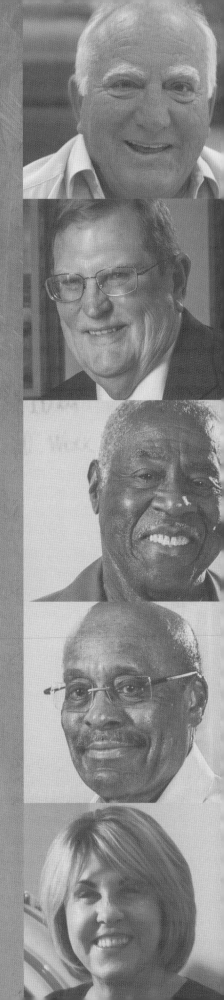

In the first fifty years of the Port's existence, the struggle was to fulfill the potential that its builders promised. During this period the discovery of oil, the growth of an international market for American cotton and grain, and the two world wars all pushed the Houston Ship Channel forward as a major economic generator, providing jobs and fostering new industries. Still, each of these developments saw, or caused, significant periods of decline in the amount of goods going up and down the Channel. Both wars initially halted much activity at the Port. Cotton exports suffered mightily during World War I. The Great Depression emptied the giant grain elevators that sat on the Port docks. World War II initially decreased traffic on the Channel, and therefore port-generated business in general, under threat of attack by enemy powers[1].

The struggles of the past half-century have been different. It is not hard to generalize, based on the words of so many men and women who have worked the Ship Channel since the 1960s, that the struggles they faced were not to imagine an entirely new and massive enterprise such as the Port and bring it into being with sweat and toil; nor did they have to face down the impact of negative market forces that decreased available work and diminished profitability. The struggle of their era was dealing with widespread socioeconomic change. From the 1950s on, as the American economy recovered from World War II, middle class prosperity became the dream of the many and not just the few. Unions, from the car industry to the waterfront, believed that blue-collar workers had proved their worth and deserved fair pay for a hard day's work. African American and Mexican American soldiers returned from defending their country with the conviction that it was time that their status and contributions be recognized as fully equal to that of all other Americans. Not far behind these emergent social agendas were the concerns of women, millions of whom were entering the workplace for the first time. To be sure, the Port and the Ship Channel, like much of the rest of the United States, were only just beginning to wrestle with the issues and come to terms with the struggles they entailed. As a result, many individual workers and entities experienced the worst and the best of these major social changes.

Of course, the most notable type of workplace struggle is the strike, a work stoppage called by organized labor. The Port of Houston experienced several in the 1930s, growing out of the Great Depression and reflecting nationwide unrest among the International Longshoremen's Association (ILA) and other unions. A major strike occurred in 1935, marked by extreme bitterness and violence over the hiring of union versus non-union workers. In the post-Depression era, "job actions" and difficult negotiations continued to be characteristic of the back and forth relations between labor and management on the Ship Channel. Nevertheless, these were minor disruptions in a three-decade period of relative calm.

However, a transformative change was in the works. In the mid-1950s a ship sailed into the Port of Houston bearing fifty-six containers filled with goods and a standard load of liquid cargo.

[1]Refer to Sibley (1968) for more comprehensive information regarding the years preceding the 1914 construction of the port and continuing on to 1968.

This was not the first use of containers on ships. Smaller versions of boxed cargo had moved in and out of the Port of Houston. But Malcolm McLean's innovation changed the nature of work on the Houston docks forever. Suddenly a world of physical laborers, accustomed to spending days to unload or load a ship, was challenged by a degree of mechanization previously unheard of. The amount of people needed for this new work, and the time necessary to complete it, foretold sweeping reductions in the workforce and job duration. This was no longer the human against human confrontation that had defined earlier labor crises, but rather a struggle pitting workers against degrees and levels of compartmentalization and mechanization impossible to compete against.

The first container ship in Houston, taken in 1956.
Courtesy of Houston Public Library, HMRC: RG1362-179

Though the introduction of containers into the Port of Houston can be fixed to a specific date, a certain event and an individual innovator, this momentous change took a while to become pervasive. It was not until 1968 that a strike comparable to what had been seen in the 1930s would slow work at the Port to a degree that was devastating to both labor and management. Work was changing drastically, and it called for strategic, even creative, responses to address the problems facing workers and the employers they served. The strike was long and costly. With the Port paralyzed for a full 106 days as negotiations were underway, all involved in the strike, from labor to management, considered the hard-won agreement to institute a Guaranteed Annual Income not so much a victory as a tough lesson. As ILA District President Benny Holland said in describing the process: "It affected me because it taught me a lot about how we should be partners in the industry; we should not be adversaries. We haven't had a strike since."

History of the International Longshoremen's Local 872 by John Biggers.
Courtesy of ILA Local, 24. Photo by Neiman Catley

Interestingly, the Gulf Coast, and especially the Port of Houston, is known for the cooperative spirit between labor and management that grew out of this difficult confrontation. While it is true that Texas is a right-to-work state, the ILA, for one, remains a strong voice for labor in the Houston Ship Channel and Union leadership is quick to point out that the new styles of work call for greater skill and training, and less physical danger and hard labor. Walt Neimand is the retired President of the West Gulf Maritime Association, which brokers the exchanges between union labor and management at the Port of Houston. He characterizes the nature of this cooperative spirit: "There have been some major advancements and a lot of the best ideas that came to the table to make us more competitive benefited the workers, but they came from the workers, and they benefited management, so it has been a mutual project, if you will, to prosper jointly."

Other labor struggles have played a part in the more recent history of the Houston Ship Channel. Until 1984, the ILA in Texas maintained segregated locals. This is an extraordinarily late date, given the fact that major civil rights legislation addressing such behavior was passed in the 1960s and became the law of the land, though sometimes forced compliance was necessary.

The long reign of segregated labor seems strangely out of place in the context of all the social progress achieved at the Port during the last quarter of the twentieth century. In fact, despite court orders, the segregated unions themselves continued to argue against a merger into the 1980s.

For some very simple and pragmatic reasons, both the black and white unions supported the status quo, even though such a stance seems counter intuitive to the social justice efforts of the era. An ILA local is structured on leadership drawn from and voted upon by the membership, and access to work is determined by seniority. Both black and white locals were invested in retaining their autonomy over leadership and seniority and did not want to dilute their separate powers through a merger. Since the brother locals had worked out an elaborate process of sharing all work that came into the Port, the segregated unions did not block access to work for one group or the other.

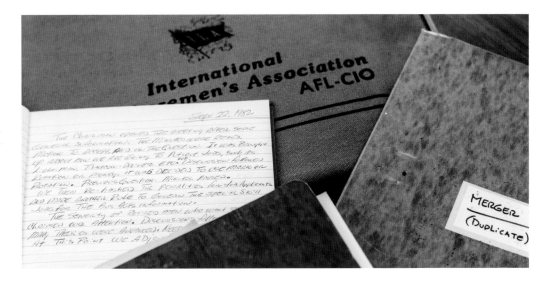

These ledgers contain the minutes of the ILA merger, as recorded by Joseph Kinch.
Photo by Neiman Catley

In Texas, a state where Jim Crow laws were plentiful, white ILA members did not object to the separate locals. Blacks, on the other hand, saw the separation differently. After receiving testimony from many black union members, Judge Garza of the U.S. District Court for the Southern District of Texas had this to say in a 1971 judgment:

> [B]y having their own unions and their own union officials, [they] have been able to better themselves by being able to hold high positions in their locals, and have been recognized in the community as a separate, powerful voice for the Negro communities, and [segregation] has attained for them and the Negro people of the community, a standing which they could not have otherwise attained[2].

[2]Montes, R. A. (2005). Working for American Rights: Black, White, and Mexican-American Dockworkers in Texas during the Great Depression (Doctoral dissertation, The University of Texas at Austin). Retrieved from http://catalog.lib.utexas.edu/

ILA Members across the Gulf Coast participate in various demonstrations.
Courtesy of Donald "Harvey" Breed

Garza's decision was overturned in 1975 by the Fifth Circuit Court of Appeals after a renewed push by the Equal Employment Opportunity Commission (EEOC). Still, the Texas unions pushed back for nine more years. In Houston, Locals 872 and 1273 realized that the continued separation was untenable. In fact, when the EEOC was about to take over the merger process, the two unions stepped up in the final hours to work out the details. Understanding that no one better comprehended their mutual concerns than their fellow ILA brothers, they began negotiations. Joseph Kinch remembers:

> *On this merger situation, I was secretary on the merger committee. We had differences and we'd sit there and talk and ironed out the differences. The EEOC did this and that, but when it came down to the real nitty-gritty we had to sit down and work it out ourselves. We had men depending on us to keep things rolling so they could work and take care of their families. Whether you like me or not makes no difference, you have got to work with me. The international constitution [of the ILA] says that any two locals in the same area doing the same work have the right to merge. We did it and went on working because we had to feed our people.*

In the long run, despite decades of resistance on both sides and from both locals, the actions to effect merger came directly from the segregated unions themselves. The committee to which Kinch refers even went so far as to develop two pages of rules of behavior to ensure peaceful relations. To the surprise of all, black and white, no major incidents occurred once the merger was in effect and all shared the same union hall.

Labor and management struggles are not an entirely unfamiliar story in the American workplace, though there has been little outright discussion of their impact on the Houston Ship Channel since the strike of 1968. The integration of the unions gets much the same silent treatment. Other labor issues during this period include discrimination: workers whose ethnicity or gender caused them to be overlooked for more highly-skilled or better-paying jobs. Adolph Postel, a thirty-eight-year employee of the Port Terminal Railroad, is eager to affirm his love for his work: "I liked it. I didn't know a better job in my lifetime." Yet, as a young Mexican American who had worked a variety of jobs before coming to the Port, he was aware that members of his community were routinely assigned the dirtier and more difficult tasks—and even life-threatening jobs like shoveling grain in a silo or unloading bananas on the docks.

Congressman Bob Eckhardt formally opening PASO voter registration headquarters in Houston. Accepting the keys to the headquarters were David Ortiz and Tony Marron.
Courtesy of Houston Public Library, HMRC: MSSO160

As it turned out, while Postel was originally hired for a largely unskilled job with the Port Terminal Railroad in 1951, he was promoted to engineer in 1970 as part of a move to advance Latinos in the organization. He and another Mexican American co-worker were the first Latinos to hold this position:

> *I was one of the first Latinos to run a locomotive. That was in 1970. Someone went to talk to somebody who wanted to know how many engineers are there. They didn't have anybody, no blacks, no Latinos;*

they put two blacks and two Latinos on the engines in 1970, and it got better and better. Now there are quite a few running locomotives. It is a good paying job, one of the better paying jobs.

It is likely that political organizers representing the interests of Texas' Mexican American community were the ones asking these questions and probing the possibility of discriminatory practices[3]. Their activism and inquiries altered the hiring and promotion habits of many industries along the Ship Channel.

Interestingly, women are still few and far between in many of the occupations plied along the ship channel. In business offices and major corporations, their presence is quite visible, but in some of the core professions on docks and ships their numbers remain low. This is no doubt due to a setting that has been for most of its history, and as much by default as by design, male-dominated and uninviting to women. Women working in physically arduous roles that once defined the work of a longshoreman, or living on a boat in close quarters among otherwise all-male crews, would face understandably difficult scenarios. On the surface, the lack of women clamoring to claim their place in either of these surroundings appears understandable. Unfortunately, we have no testimony from the few women who may have taken up this challenge.

Yet, the workplaces themselves played a part in distancing women. Vidal Knight remembers her years working alongside her husband as a co-owner of a towing business:

He rode the boat full time. I had a full time job, a baby and an eight-year-old. So it was my responsibility to take him supplies because he couldn't really get off of the boat. This was totally unheard of, for a woman to get close to the docks. There were signs posted everywhere saying, "No Women or Children Allowed Near the Docks." The sign didn't mean anything to men; it meant something to me.

But despite the fact that certain companies and corporations created thoughtless and discriminatory barriers, Knight notes that many of the people involved—the workers themselves— understood her dilemma and went out of their way to assist.

Some of the men were just looking after me or looking out for me, so I could never say I had it so tough because I was a woman. I would drive my truck down to the docks and stand at the gate, rain or wind or whatever the conditions were. The people at the refinery would be kind enough to send someone up to the gate, get my truck and drive it down to the boat. And the crew would unload and would drive the truck back to me. Under no circumstances was I allowed to enter the guard gate.

[3] GI Forum, Raza Unida, Mexican American Youth Organization, League of United Latin American Citizens, Civic Action Committee, Political Association of Spanish-Speaking Organizations, Mexican American Education Council and the Association for the Advancement of Mexican Americans

Holly Cooper, a Houston Pilot for twenty years now, was a pioneering female presence in a professional association that is highly competitive and rigorous in every aspect of its selection process. Sometimes assumptions and antiquated thinking were the biggest difficulties she had to overcome. Pilots do not get an introduction to the crew when they meet a ship in the channel, so unknowing captains can betray their own prejudices:

> *If you board down in Galveston, you have the pilot boat come alongside and you grab hold of the ladder. You climb up and the pilot boat takes off. This happened many, many times to me—I climbed on up and all of a sudden the pilot boat takes off and they go, "Oh, the pilot, the pilot, we need the pilot. Bring the pilot back!" … You have to tell them, "No, I am the pilot. I really am." There are times when I walk up to the bridge and they all just look at me and then they watch me intently for a while and then they finally start to relax.*

And she had her own personal struggle to overcome—a hurdle created not by discriminatory practices or prejudicial behavior, but rather by the realities of contemporary life. Even older pilots, ones whose wives may never have entered the workplace, talk of the demands that their occupation placed on them and their families. Holly comments on the tough act of balancing life on the job with life at home.

> *If you look at how many women have a maritime background, the odds are that very few women have wanted to go to sea or have stuck it out. [Family life] has something to do with it. I postponed having a son until late in life. I was probably the first pregnant female as a pilot out here—I worked through seven-and-a-half months. It's funny because most of my fellow pilots didn't know I was pregnant. They just thought I was putting on weight.* ▌

BENNY
HOLLAND

From 'HOT-BODY' LABOR
to a SKILLED INDUSTRY

AFTER WORLD WAR II, THE AMERICAN WORKFORCE SAW GREAT CHANGES DUE TO ADVANCES IN TECHNOLOGY AND MECHANIZATION. THE PORT ENVIRONMENT WAS NO EXCEPTION—OVER TIME, IT WAS DRASTICALLY TRANSFORMED BY INNOVATIONS THAT REDUCED THE NEED FOR DIRECT MANUAL LABOR. THE INTRODUCTION OF AUTOMATION AND CONTAINERIZATION DURING THE 1950S MEANT THAT CARGO WAS INCREASINGLY GOING TO BE MOVED BY CRANES IN LARGE METAL CONTAINERS RATHER THAN ON THE BACKS OF HUMAN LABORERS. IN THE FOLLOWING INTERVIEW EXCERPT, BENNY HOLLAND IS A VENERABLE FIGURE, A LONGTIME MEMBER OF THE INTERNATIONAL LONGSHOREMEN'S ASSOCIATION (ILA), RECOGNIZED, ON THE GULF COAST AS WELL AS NATIONALLY, AS A MAJOR LEADER OF THIS UNION. HERE HOLLAND RECOUNTS HIS PERSONAL EXPERIENCE WORKING THE DOCKS IN THE DAYS WHEN COTTON WAS HOUSTON'S MOST IMPORTANT CARGO AND WAS HANDLED ENTIRELY AS PIECEWORK. HE SPEAKS OF THE TEAMWORK AND THE FRATERNAL SPIRIT THAT WERE NECESSARY FOR SUCH RIGOROUS AND PUNISHING WORK.

We loaded cotton with a fifteen-man gang. It was two guys running the winch and a gang foreman signaling the winchmen. There were four guys on the dock that would send cotton into the hold. They would just hook it up and put it on the slack, and the winchmen would pull it into the hold. Then there were four men on the end shore and four men on the offshore side. They would take these bales and roll them into the hold and stack them. Work was so hard that they would alternate every two or two-and-a-half hours. You would stay in the hold for five hours and go on the docks for two-and-a-half hours, and then you would rotate. A lot of times, if there were older guys that I knew had a hard day, I would just say, "Just stay out there on the wharf and I will do your work." A lot of guys did that; it was how we tried to take care of each other.

After I was established, I became a foreman, not a gang foreman but a walking foreman. A walking foreman would be ahead of the ship on his end. I had four gangs. I would tell the gang foreman where to go and what holds and what we were going to put in these holds and what hatch was going to go here and whether we were going to be in the lower hold or the 'tween deck or whatever. We would explain to them how to work a ship and I would keep track of the tonnage and make sure they were doing the proper tonnage. I did that for a while and then the guys came to me and wanted me to run for office [in the labor union]. So, I decided to run and had to give up the foreman's job to run for Assistant Business Agent from 1968 to '69.

> ..., if there were older guys
> that I knew had a hard day,
> I would just say, "Just stay out there
> on the wharf and I will do your work."
> A lot of guys did that; it was how
> we tried to take care of each other.

BY THE 1960S, EMPLOYERS WERE OFFERING FEWER UNSKILLED JOBS AND WORK ASSIGNMENTS BECAUSE CONTAINERIZATION OF CARGO REDUCED THE TIME IT TOOK TO LOAD AND UNLOAD A SHIP BY A FACTOR OF TEN AND DEMANDED A HIGHER LEVEL OF KNOWLEDGE ON THE PART OF THE WORKER. WHEN BENNY HOLLAND RAN FOR OFFICE IN 1968, HE WAS ENTERING THE UNION LEADERSHIP AT THE APEX OF THAT CHANGE. THE UNION WAS STRUGGLING TO KEEP PORT WORKERS' LIVELIHOODS AFLOAT AMIDST THE AUTOMATION OF THE INDUSTRY, WHILE MANAGEMENT FOCUSED ON HEIGHTENED EFFICIENCY AND COST CUTTING TO REMAIN COMPETITIVE. THESE CHANGES, AND THE POLARIZING PERSPECTIVES THEY BRED BETWEEN LABOR AND INDUSTRY MANAGEMENT ON THE SHIP CHANNEL, DOMINATED PORT LIFE IN 1968, WHEN THE ILA ORGANIZED A LABOR STRIKE, BENNY WAS ON THE FRONTLINE. HIS MEMORIES OF THE STRIKE NEGOTIATIONS ILLUMINATE THE CHANGES THAT PROVOKED THE CONFLICT.

The strike was about automation. That was the turning point in the industry. It took our industry from what I like to call a "hot-body" industry—where you could get anybody to throw a hundred-pound sack of flour and learn how to not hurt himself—to a skilled industry. Anybody can throw a hundred-pound sack of flour if he is strong, but now we need to have a really skilled, talented person run a seven-million-dollar crane to pick up a million dollars worth of cargo in a container and put it on a ship without hurting somebody or damaging the cargo. So it is a totally different workforce—and that was the start of the industry evolving from a "hot-body" to a skilled industry. The negotiations during the 1968 labor strike were all centered on that move and change.

We knew that automation was going to eliminate jobs. The number one stumbling block was that the International had established a guaranteed annual income. They said to management, "You are going to get all these savings by eliminating all of these jobs. We want you to guarantee a certain amount of jobs called the Guaranteed Annual Income (GAI), so a guy can get paid if he lost his job, and he will get a certain amount of money every week." Most meetings were held in the Galvez Hotel in Galveston and some meetings were held here in the Helena Hotel in Houston. We were negotiating for the whole of the West Gulf, from Lake Charles to Brownsville, Texas, and we were negotiating with the West Gulf Maritime Association, a group of employers. They had a spokesperson at that time; his name was Bill Arnett. Buddy Raspberry was negotiating for us. We had a team of seven of us sitting behind Buddy working with him, just as Bill Arnett had a team of seven stevedores sitting behind him. We were the ones at the table constantly. Behind us, in another room, each local had representatives on the contract committee and each company had representatives. We would do all the infighting, take it out to them and then we would caucus.

> *The number one stumbling block was ... the guaranteed annual income.*

We took on all issues from A to Z. The number one stumbling block was the guaranteed annual income and, of course, wages and benefits, because we knew we were going to lose a lot of man-hours due to automation. We had to protect our welfare and pension fund and we wanted to make sure our guys were compensated for the jobs lost. On the other hand, management was protecting their customers, and a lot of customers did not want to guarantee income. I can understand that, but we had to protect our guys, too—we had to make sure their concerns were addressed—and management wanted to make sure their customers' concerns were addressed. So, there were very difficult negotiations. Both sides had, in my opinion, very strong points. From a management standpoint it would be difficult to pay a guy not to work. From my point, I can't see a guy giving up the job he had for a really long time, the job he hopes his son will have. Both sides had very good arguments and it took people to come together and make it work. It was a long, drawn-out affair that lasted 106 days and finally we prevailed in winning a GAI package.

THE 1968 LABOR STRIKE DID INDEED RESULT IN GUARANTEED WORKER COMPENSATION. BENNY HOLLAND WAS INTIMATELY INVOLVED IN THIS NEGOTIATION PROCESS AND NOW REFLECTS ON THE PERSONAL FINANCIAL TOLL HE PAID, BUT ALSO THE DAMAGE SUSTAINED ON BOTH SIDES OF THE STRUGGLE. HIS WORDS REFLECT THOSE OF MANY RECENTLY INTERVIEWED VETERANS OF THE STRIKE:

During the strike, I didn't work at all because I was on call or standby for negotiations and meetings that were on anytime over those 106 days. A lot of the guys who worked on the dock went to work as ironworkers and had other side jobs in order to earn some money. Unfortunately for me, for those four months I did not get to work at all. I had a wife and two children at home and my wife didn't work, so it was kind of tough. It was a great learning experience because it taught me a lot about life and how important it is to make things work rather than fight over things. I don't think anyone won when you look at a 106-day strike. We were out three months without a paycheck. We earned it back at a dollar-an-hour raise or fifty-cent-an-hour raise, but it took a lot of years to get back three months of salary. I don't think management won—we lost a few customers because for three months they had to get their cargo to shelf some way. They lost customers. I don't think it was a win-win, and we have learned from that. We haven't had a strike since.

> *It was an experience for me to learn that we did much better as partners than we did as adversaries.*

We all have a common goal, to move the product from the manufacturer to the consumer. Whether you own the ship, or you own the Port, whether you are a longshoreman that loads and unloads the ship, whether you are a truck driver that drives the truck from the Port to the consumer, we all have a job to do, and that is to deliver the product from the manufacturer to the consumer. So, we all become partners and we should work as partners. It was an experience for me to learn that we did much better as partners than we did as adversaries. ▌

Interview conducted by Pat Jasper on September 9, 2011
Photo by Lou Vest.

WALT
NEIMAND

At the BARGAINING TABLE

FEW PEOPLE COULD HAVE IMAGINED HOW, IN 1956, A REFITTED OIL TANKER CARRYING FIFTY-EIGHT SHIPPING CONTAINERS FROM NEWARK TO HOUSTON WOULD BE THE FIRST STEP IN THE CREATION OF AN ENORMOUS INDUSTRY WITH GLOBAL REACH[1]. SOME HAVE EVEN GONE AS FAR AS TO FRAME THE ADVENT OF CONTAINERIZATION AS THE ENABLER OF GLOBALIZATION. HOWEVER, MUCH LESS HAS BEEN SAID OF THE LOCALIZED, COMPLEX NEGOTIATIONS THAT NEEDED TO TAKE PLACE BETWEEN WORKERS AND BUSINESSES—BETWEEN LABOR AND MANAGEMENT—IN ORDER TO TRANSITION TO THIS NEW INTERNATIONAL MARKETPLACE. WALT NEIMAND GIVES HIS PERSPECTIVE ON THE PROCESS AS THE FORMER PRESIDENT AND CHIEF EXECUTIVE OF THE WEST GULF MARITIME ASSOCIATION, THE ENTITY THAT NEGOTIATES AND ADMINISTERS LABOR AGREEMENTS WITH THE UNION, THE INTERNATIONAL LONGSHOREMEN'S ASSOCIATION.

Here, at the West Gulf Maritime Association (WGMA), we have three people in labor relations for eight ports[2].

We represent management: the carriers that operate the vessels, the agents that deal with the vessels, the governmental agencies and the labor that work in an area. West Gulf Maritime does not load vessels, but works for multiple companies that are all members of the association. We do labor relations and we also do payrolling. We conduct training to meet all the government requirements and teach workers about automation, which is now more and more critical in our business. Also, we do safety and security work on behalf of management and government relations—maritime affairs both on the state and federal level on behalf of our members in the maritime industry.

The West Gulf Maritime Association is the one that produces payroll checks. The five different employers that a longshoreman has worked for in a week reimburse us. Workers get one check stub on a West Gulf Maritime check and, when I was president, my name would be on

[1]Levinson, Marc. 2008. *The Box: How the Shipping Container Made the World Smaller and the World Economy Bigger*. Princeton, N.J.: Princeton University Press.
[2]The Port of Houston Authority, Port of Brownsville, Port of Corpus Christi, Port of Galveston, Port of Freeport, Port of Texas City, Port of Port Arthur, and Port of Lake Charles.

the check. The Association only does payroll for union workers under collective bargaining agreements. If you asked a longshore worker in Houston, "Who do you work for?" he might say the ILA, which is his labor union because he is dispatched out of a hiring hall every day, but normally, they would say West Gulf Maritime. In Houston, workers don't have to be a member of the union; they can just work under the general contract because this is a right-to-work state. The non-union workers represent a million to a million and a half man-hours, which is significant; but the union represents over five million man-hours.

The ILA here was very militant at one time. People shot at one another during bargaining and came armed to the table. By the time I came here in 1980 [the tensions between labor and management] had greatly subsided. Management and labor have learned that only by mutual cooperation can both prosper. We worked very hard at that. Since then, there have been some major advancements, and a lot of the best ideas that came to the table to make us more competitive came from workers. These ideas benefited the workers and benefited management, so it has been a mutual project to prosper jointly. So we have not had major strikes and problems of that nature since I was involved.

We have only had one major work stoppage since I have been here, and that was limited to just one port. It was a series of issues over a year and half when the union was trying to shut down new operators that were working non-union. So instead of stopping something, you had to adjust and think, "How am I going to compete with it?" Really, that's what changed the attitudes. If you could no longer afford to go to impasse, then you had to figure out solutions. If they didn't work, you had to change mid-contract and continue to work at making the changes necessary to survive. So there were constant negotiations, but a lot of it frankly was sitting down and saying, "Here is a problem, let's look at ideas that we all have on how we can confront and overcome this

problem, that would be to our mutual benefit." For example, there were negotiations that came up with a pay guarantee, so that if you were available for work, and you were there for so many years in the industry, you were going to be paid until you died or retired. This was never used to any great degree at all except in a few small ports because there was more work than there had been before. That money was actually paid in bonuses to the workers. Sometimes labor prevailed and sometimes management did, but for the most part everyone survived.

> [*Management and labor have learned that only by mutual cooperation can both prosper.*]

I think both the labor and management didn't look forward to the bargaining. It was what we were paid to do and we were successful in accomplishing that, but we had some hard times—some screaming and hollering—but I don't think any of us ever severed our own personal relationships. I still exchange Christmas cards with families of people I worked with and still see them on a somewhat regular basis. You can't have it get personal—that just doesn't work.

WHILE ALL INTERNATIONAL PORTS HAVE HAD TO ADJUST TO THE RESHAPING OF THE SHIPPING INDUSTRY BEGINNING IN THE 1950S, THE NEGOTIATIONS AND RELATIONSHIPS THAT HAVE ARISEN BETWEEN UNIONS AND SHIPPING COMPANIES HAVE DIFFERED MARKEDLY FROM PORT TO PORT. WALT NEIMAND REFLECTS ON THIS SHIFT AND HOW WORKING ON THE WEST COAST HAS INFORMED HIS WORK WITH WGMA.

Automation and containerization did not turn out the way labor and management thought it would—it actually created more jobs than it destroyed. The jobs were much more highly skilled and required a lot more capital investment and equipment. We had such an increase in shipping and cargo that we had more jobs than we thought we would. For example, here in the West Gulf area, there is still a lot of break bulk cargo. The man-hours here are about sixty percent automated work. In comparison, over on the West Coast it is well over ninety percent. So the work has changed, but the number of man-hours did not decline as was forecasted. So now there are people who are much more highly skilled that do a lot more work with better productivity. So the salaries and fringe benefits for the workers have increased dramatically.

Pacific Maritime has a very similar role to the West Gulf [Maritime Association]. They have an outside group that does their government relations and lobbying work. I was in labor relations there and basically dealt with labor unions. The atmosphere was very adversarial. The ILW [International Longshore and Warehouse Union] on the West Coast is a very militant union, even today. They have virtually no non-union competition, which is fairly different than what you see on the Gulf Coast. They represent the warehouse, the longshoremen, the clerks and the walking foremen. An individual that jumped ship from Australia—Harry Bridges—organized them. He was very adamant in his views of the classes in the United States and what working people needed to do for themselves. There were constant work stoppages. Out there in just Southern California alone we had six ports and we had over one hundred arbitrations a year. There was an eight-step grievance procedure to keep ships from being shut down. It was a very arduous type of work assignment, but it was interesting too.

It can get arduous and it can get tiring for both sides. Whereas shooting at one another (as it used to happen) wasn't going to get us anywhere, it is tiring trying to find solutions that the ILA can sell to the people they represent and the WGMA can sell to the people we represent. For example, when I came down here they had a job security program. They wanted to guarantee workers income if they had been here so many years. The Job

Security Program (JSP) had to be financed by the employers. Then we had a major fall-out in work in Houston, the largest port, in the mid-1980s. The amount of money that we had put away was enough to take care of this forecasted need for a year to a year-and-a-half, but when Houston went down it was completely spent in three months. So we had a situation where we had a contractual requirement to meet and we didn't have the money. We sat down with the labor union—they had every right to shut us down—and basically they had to agree that if we shut down there would be even less work. So we had to do away with that contract section and come up with other solutions to create jobs. They walked away from what was in writing—and legally required for us to pay—in order for us to survive and work. On the West Coast, I had never seen that.

> *What I learned is that you have to try and understand what you are talking about from the other's point of view.*

Right now, unfortunately or fortunately, depending on one's political point of view, you have fewer and fewer unions. The only growth in unions is in government work. The number of labor unions and the labor bargaining that you have has greatly diminished over the years. So you have fewer people going into that field and you have fewer and fewer percentage of the workforce as union workers. What I learned is that you have to try and understand what you are talking about from the other's point of view. When I went into the labor relations industry, it was growing and now it is not; that is something that needs to be recognized. ∎

Interview conducted by Elizabeth Peterson on January 11, 2012.
Photo by Jack Potts.

JOSEPH **KINCH** &
HOMER **GUILLORY**

WE *had to* SIT DOWN *and* *work it out* OURSELVES

WATERFRONT WORKERS ARE ON THE FRONTLINE OF ALL ACTIVITY ALONG THE SHIP CHANNEL; SO WHEN A SUBSTANTIAL CHANGE TRANSPIRES IN THAT SETTING, IT RESONATES POWERFULLY AMONG THE LONGSHOREMEN, WHO CARRY THE NEWS TO THE SURROUNDING COMMUNITIES. ALL FORMS OF CHANGE HAVE AN IMPACT—FROM WEATHER CONDITIONS, TO TECHNOLOGICAL INNOVATIONS, TO SHIFTING SOCIAL RELATIONSHIPS AMONG WORKERS. AN INTERVIEW WITH OLD FRIENDS AND FELLOW ILA MEN, HOMER GUILLORY AND JOSEPH KINCH, SHEDS LIGHT ON THE TRANSFORMATIONS THAT THE PORT OF HOUSTON HAS UNDERGONE FROM ITS EARLIEST DAYS AND EVEN BEFORE THE ESTABLISHMENT OF THE PORT AS AN OFFICIAL ENTITY. KINCH STARTS BY SHARING SOME OF THE STORIES PASSED ON TO HIM BY HIS GRANDFATHER REGARDING THE EARLY UNION DAYS IN HOUSTON.

JOSEPH KINCH: *My grandfather was born in 1876, the same year Custer got slaughtered at Little Bighorn. He left Louisiana about 1898 and moved to Galveston and started working on the waterfront. When the news came to Galveston that Houston was starting a port, him and Mundy Albright and Saul Ashford came up and established the International Longshoremen's union here. The group came and helped establish the 872 local [labor union] in Houston. Once they did, the ships started coming in. The workers would have to stand by. They would call them on the phone from Galveston, tell them the ship just passed a point and it would be on the way. They would be waiting on it when it came. The first ship that came in was a Spanish ship, which docked up at City Dock 1 or 2, the More Eagle. That was the beginning of the work here in the Port of Houston.*

After this, they worked downtown as long as they could, until it got crowded. Then they moved out here on Memphis and 75th Street. This is where they did the hiring. Then they started working on the City Dock 4. They had built the Turning Basin and ships were getting too big to go down Buffalo Bayou to the downtown ports. In Houston, now you only really see work from City Dock 4 to 32, because City Docks 1 through 5 were in downtown. They accommodated smaller ships. When ships started getting bigger, they had to move, dredge the Turning Basin and put the docks up here.

AS WATERFRONT WORKERS, THEY KNEW THE RIGOR OF MANUAL LABOR AND SAW IT CHANGE OVER THE YEARS, WITH AUTOMATION AND THE CONTAINERIZATION OF CARGO. NO MATTER THE NATURE OF THE CHANGES, GUILLORY AND KINCH LIVED THE LESSONS OF THE WORK AND APPLIED THEM DAY-TO-DAY. IN THE GIVE AND TAKE OF THIS INTERVIEW, WE HEAR HOW THESE LESSONS PLAYED A PART IN THEIR WORK AND SOMETHING OF HOW FELLOW WORKERS SHARED INFORMATION. CAUTION, SAFETY AND PRUDENCE WERE ALWAYS A NECESSARY PART OF THE JOB—BEFORE AND AFTER AUTOMATION.

JOSEPH KINCH: *Everything at that time was not in containers; everything was done by hand. Some of the sacks weighed more than I did. I was lucky to have strength enough to pick them up with a partner. After I got physically used to it, there was nothing to it, but you had to get physically used to the work, especially if you were working in the hold. It was hot down there, and the air was stagnant. You had to know how to drink water. If you drank water, you had to flush it in your mouth, spit it out, then take your drink and go back to work. You don't drink a whole lot of cold water at one time or you're going to cramp.*

So we had to learn these things, and learn what to wear in the hold. If you wore a t-shirt, you were not going to last long; you were going to burn out. If you get you a sweatshirt, and sweat and get that sweatshirt wet, then you were all right. You could make that summer with that sweatshirt. But it was a learning process of things that were small and common to people that were older because they had to work in the heat, so they knew and they would teach you, and if you paid attention to them, you could make a day.

> *Some of the sacks weighed more than I did. I was lucky to have strength enough to pick them up with a partner.*

HOMER GUILLORY: *Containers came in the late 1960s. They were not shaped like the containers today, but more or less like a square box, eight feet tall. When that experiment proved to be advantageous to the industry, they shaped them to the size they are now, twenty by forty feet to accommodate more cargo in one lift. That was the beginning of automation, to my knowledge.*

JOSEPH KINCH: *Back in the earlier days, everything was steam driven. The Japanese had the best steam winches, the German and Japanese. I learned how to drive on steam winches. Steam would pick up most anything, but* *if you didn't use it right, you'd hurt someone. You had to be skilled.*

HOMER GUILLORY: *Piecework cargo, whether you were unloading or loading, came in one load at a time. You had eight men in the hold and you had four men on port side. You might have sacks, boxes and general cargo. As the ships got modern, getting away from steam winches toward the container phase, you could have more tonnage and the piecework faded out in the early 1980s. It came back around 2000, because of the city docks, but it's mostly automation now.*

> *You had to know how to drink water. If you drank water, you had to flush it in your mouth, spit it out, then take your drink and go back to work.*

IN THE LATE 1960S, IT BECAME A CONCERN THAT IT WAS NOT ONLY THE KIND OF WORK THAT WAS CHANGING FOR LONGSHOREMAN; IT WAS ALSO THE AMOUNT OF WORK. MANAGEMENT AND LABOR HAD TO FIND COMMON GROUND ON THIS ISSUE, BUT THE PROCESS OF GETTING THERE TOOK TIME AND A TOLL.

HOMER GUILLORY: *The strike [of 1968] had to do with contract disagreement between management and labor. The wages were the biggest argument. We went on strike, using that as a tool to get what we wanted in monetary raises. This is a common tool that organized labor uses. It lasted 106 days before management came around to give us some of what we wanted. We haven't had a major strike since then. We've had some walk-offs, but nothing major. We've always been able to agree on something contract-wise that would benefit both sides.*

I'm a third generation. My dad was a longshoreman probably with Mr. Kinch. I came under Mr. Kinch. I worked for him as a laborer, him being a liaison

between management and labor; they called that a walking foreman.

After the strike, we started utilizing the advantages that we got from the strike in our contract agreements. The objective was to attract customers and bring the work here. That's what we do now—provide good labor for our customers. It's been working. We did have a decline in 1983, where we priced ourselves out of a job with contract negotiations. Management couldn't afford to pay what we were asking. Non-union workers were right on our heels to offer cheaper labor, so we had to compete with them or go down the drain. We were at top dollar at eighteen dollars an hour. We took a cut back to fourteen dollars to keep what we had to compete with non-union. It was rough. Some guys stayed, some left. The ones that stayed built the industry back on our side, the labor side. It's always been the debate between management and labor, which we've survived. We have benefits, insurance, retirement—second to none in the realm of common labor.

AS THIRD-GENERATION LONGSHOREMEN, GUILLORY AND KINCH HEARD MANY STORIES ABOUT THE CONDITIONS UNDER WHICH THEIR FATHERS AND GRANDFATHERS WORKED. THEIR TESTIMONY IS AN IMPORTANT PART OF UNDERSTANDING HOW A SYSTEM OF SEGREGATED UNIONS DEVELOPED AND SOME OF THE REASONS THEY REMAINED IN PLACE SO LONG.

JOSEPH KINCH: *I don't know all the reasoning [behind forming a specifically African American union]. I think it's because most of the white guys didn't want to work this type of manual labor, and they had to have somebody unload the ships, so the African Americans took it. The 1273 local got established by way of 872. When they got established, they would have the forward end of the ship and we would have the aft end of the ship. Normally, the ships at the time had two hatches that were aft and three hatches that were forward. They were generally pretty generous in giving one another a break. If we had the forward end, they would work the aft end.*

To keep the work based on half-and-half, they would alternate the ends of the ships with the blacks and the whites. As soon as things were pretty good, sometimes the blacks would work together with the whites, until the Ku Klux Klan got into it. These are the things my grandfather told me. The KKK didn't want the whites working with the blacks and the blacks working with the whites. So this is when we had one end of the ship and the whites had the other end of the ship.

The 872 local was the mother local. When the white people found out that blacks were making more money than they were on menial jobs, then they wanted to come and get "a piece of the rock," as the saying goes. By us being benevolent people, we let them come on. As soon as the KKK got into it, they said, "You don't need to be working with those blacks." This is when they came up with the separate locals. Other than that, they probably would have been together. My grandfather told me the Klan caused all the mess in the Port. That caused there to be two locals in this Port. That's all I can go by.

The eventual merger of the locals in the early 1980s was by court order, but the process was slowed by the locals themselves. Over time, the separate locals for blacks and whites had fostered traditions of autonomy and safeguarded control over seniority in a manner that secured protections for their distinct communities. Surrendering these protections was a difficult concession for any local to make.

HOMER GUILLORY: *I do remember that after the locals merged there were still segregated signs in the restroom area, white and colored, in the warehouses, even in the warehouses that went up after 1957-58. They started adding those to the docks, from City Dock 16 until they got to 32, maybe in the late 1970s. Those segregated signs were still in the restroom. They also had water fountains in the back of the warehouses, white and colored, until somebody made a move to desegregate. It might have been the law that was passed. They came down after that.*

JOSEPH KINCH: *It wasn't until the EEOC[1] got into the whole thing that desegregation came about. The signs came down and then we began to talk about a merger to get within the law. We were breaking the law by having two separate locals. In order to get within the law, we had to merge.*

> As soon as things were pretty good, sometimes the blacks would work together with the whites, until the Ku Klux Klan got into it.

WHILE THE SEPARATE BLACK AND WHITE LOCALS HAD PRAGMATIC REASONS TO STICK WITH THE EXISTING SET-UP, THE WORKERS KNEW THAT SOCIAL PROGRESS HUNG IN THE BALANCE. ULTIMATELY BY CEDING THEIR SEPARATE POWER, THEY BUILT A STRONGER UNION AND ADVANCED CONDITIONS FOR WORKERS IN GENERAL. AND THEY DID IT THEMSELVES, IN FACE-TO-FACE MEETINGS, THROUGH HARD-NOSED REALISM AND PRACTICALITY.

HOMER GUILLORY: *The first day when the unions came together in a common hiring hall, it was predicted that blood was going to run out of this hall, but it didn't happen. Those that did not want to abide by the law or integrate left. There was a lot of friction, but I don't remember fistfights. Cooler heads prevailed and we worked together and got this thing organized to where we are right now. We had a cooling off period, an initial period where we maintained union officials on each side working together until we came up a common election. Up to that point, it was the guys who understood what this thing was all about ran the show. Anyone who went against the grain had to go.*

JOSEPH KINCH: *On this merger situation, I was secretary on the merger committee. I still have the information. We had differences and we'd sit there and talk and*

[1]Equal Employment Opportunity Commission

ironed out the differences. I kept the minutes. Under the international constitution, the union in New York was set to send representatives to merge the unions, but they stayed out of it and let the EEOC handle it. The EEOC did this and that, but when it came down to the real nitty-gritty we had to sit down and work it out ourselves. We had men depending on us to keep things rolling so they could work and take care of their families. This is one thing that I stressed in the meeting. We've got to get together to feed our families. Whether you like me or not makes no difference, you have got to work with me. The international constitution [of the ILA] says that any two locals in the same area doing the same work have the right to merge. We did it and went on working because we had to feed our people. That's the way I felt about it. ▌

Interview conducted by Pat Jasper on April 19, 2014.
Photo by Jack Potts.

VIDAL KNIGHT

NO WOMEN *or* *children* ALLOWED

NOT UNLIKE MANY, VIDAL KNIGHT AND HER HUSBAND FELL INTO THEIR OCCUPATIONS AS OWNERS OF A TOWING COMPANY ON THE SHIP CHANNEL. HER HUSBAND RAN THE BUSINESS BUT SHE PLAYED A KEY ROLE FROM THE BEGINNING. IT WAS DEMANDING FOR BOTH OF THEM AND OFTEN DIFFICULT FOR HER AS A WOMAN TO SHARE THE WORK OF KEEPING A FAMILY BUSINESS MOVING FORWARD.

My husband actually started off in the marine business. He worked as a deckhand to help himself through school. When he got out of the Navy, we went to Austin so that he could attend UT. His part-time job was as a deckhand, dredging out Town Lake. So we got started from him having these two little deckhand jobs. We had some friends who had a boat, and he came home one day and said he was going to buy the boat from his friend. Our first job was with this little 245-horsepower boat with the Western Towing Company that is now part of Kirby Inland Marine, which was then part of Dixie Carriers.

He rode the boat full time. I had a full-time job, a baby and an eight-year-old. So, it was my responsibility to take him supplies because he couldn't really get off of the boat. This was totally unheard of, for a woman to get close to the docks. There were signs posted everywhere saying, "No Women or Children Allowed Near the Docks." The sign didn't mean anything to men; it meant something to me. The two signs that I distinctly remember were at Shell Oil and the Western Towing Company. There was a gentleman at Western Towing Company who did not like women even getting close.

BUT AS IS FREQUENTLY THE CASE ON THE PORT, KNIGHT WAS ABLE TO DO HER JOB WITH THE HELP OF SYMPATHETIC CO-WORKERS. AS THEIR BUSINESS GREW, SO DID HER ROLE. AND, EVENTUALLY, HER STATUS AS A FEMALE BUSINESS OWNER ACTUALLY RECEIVED POSITIVE RECOGNITION WHEN SHE WAS NAMED TO THE BOARD OF CHROMALLOY AMERICAN CORPORATION.

But some of the men were just looking after me or looking out for me, so I could never say I had it so tough because I was a woman. I would drive my truck down to the docks and stand at the gate, rain or wind or whatever the conditions were. The people at the refinery would be kind enough to send someone up to the gate, get my truck, and drive it down to the boat. And the crew would unload and would drive the truck back to me. Under no circumstances was I allowed to enter the guard gate. Today, one of the things that really gets to my mind is that at Shell Oil there is now a minority lady as the guard keeper. So times have sure changed! It was very difficult; I just didn't know any better. All I wanted to do was do my job and to take care of our investment. I never got to ride the boats.

We then bought another secondhand boat. By that time, we had established a relationship, so we had a crew for the first boat that we could depend on. My husband could drive the other boat. I had to quit my insurance job and work full-time taking care of the supplies and the vessels. Then we built new boats and our company grew. The biggest fleet we ever had was nine vessels. The client base was Union Carbide, Exxon and the Valley Line. The Valley Line was dry cargo; Union Carbide and Exxon were wet cargo or chemicals. We had one boat that worked for Dow Chemical for fifteen years. We had two boats that worked for Stolt-Nielsen for ten years. Our boats did a great job.

We then sold it to Chromalloy American Corporation, an American corporation out of St. Louis, Missouri. We signed contracts to stay on as employees, which was part of the sale agreement. Then they called me and asked me if I wanted to be on their board of directors. This was in 1977-78, because corporations wanted to have a female presence. So for five years, I would go to St. Louis once a month and attend a board meeting, which was a high experience for me and for the guys as well. There were eleven guys and me. It turned out to be such an ed-

ucation. They couldn't have treated me any more nicely than they did. They accepted some of my input.

> We had some friends who had a boat, and he came home one day and said he was going to buy the boat from his friend.

KNIGHT DISCUSSES THE DIFFERENCE BETWEEN RIVER BOATS, CANAL PUSH BOATS AND HARBOR TUGS AND, IN DOING SO, POINTS TO THE INTERCONNECTEDNESS OF PORTS ALONG THE GULF COAST. HER COMMENTS ALSO REFER TO THE "OIL BUST" OF THE EARLY 1980S THAT DEVASTATED MANY BUSINESSES IN THE REGION, ESPECIALLY SMALL ONES. AND, FINALLY, SHE DISCUSSES THE LOSS OF HER HUSBAND AND HER SUCCESSFUL STRUGGLE TO TEACH HERSELF THE INS AND OUTS OF THE BUSINESS AND PULL IT TOGETHER ON HER OWN.

That was interesting because what we did was on the canal and what they did was on the river, so it was totally different. The agreement between ourselves and Chromalloy was that their riverboats would drop their barges, with destinations in the canal, either in New Orleans or Baton Rouge. We then would pick them up and bring them into the canal to their destination in Houston or Brownsville or wherever. In 1980, business got bad and barges were tied up everywhere because there wasn't any work for any of them. So Chromalloy American Corporation closed our office here in Houston.

In 1983, we started another company and started from one boat again. My husband took care of the operations part of the boat as best as he could. Even though I knew all about crew changes and I knew the crew and knew how to do all of that, I didn't know a lot about the engines. My husband died in 1990 and left me with the boats, but I continued to run that business for five years. Just two months after he died, one of the boats knocked a propeller off and it was gone! So, first thing I had to figure out was where the spare wheels were. I had no idea where he had them! After being in the shipyard for twelve to fourteen hours, I figured out where the propellers were. One of them had to be re-machined. There was a machine shop that we had used for years and they did it wrong so the minute we put the boat back in the water it started vibrating. It didn't take me too long to figure out that there was something wrong with the propeller to cause that and we had to fix it all over again.

I used to go to Stewart and Stevenson or Caterpillar and learn as much as I could because I was so afraid. I didn't trust anybody to change the oil or check the engines. Some of them tried to pull the wool over my eyes, so after two to three months I said, "Gene's dead, so we are going to do it my way. It might not be right, but if it is not, we will just redo it." The day my husband died, I went down to each boat and told them what had happened and I said, "The company is not for sale. If you want to work for me, with me, you are more than welcome to stay; but if you don't, I understand." Not one person left. For five years, I was taking care of the boats and doing my insurance job. For eight months, I did it myself with almost no help and that's the only way you can learn, by not depending on somebody else.

KNIGHT IS NOW THE OWNER OF MAXIMGROUP, A MARINE INSURANCE COMPANY AND BROKERAGE FIRM. SHE EXPLAINS HOW SHE USED HER EDUCATION, RESOURCEFULNESS AND KNOWLEDGE OF THE MARITIME INDUSTRY TO START YET ANOTHER CRUCIAL BUSINESS—INSURING MARITIME BUSINESSES. ACCIDENTS CAN HAPPEN, AND THEY DO. BY THE TIME SHE EMBARKED ON THIS SEGMENT OF HER CAREER, HER EXPERIENCE WAS UNPARALLELED FOR A WOMAN IN HER FIELD.

I had stopped doing insurance work when I went to work with my husband full-time, but I realized that there were people peddling insurance and they had no idea what they were doing. They didn't know what a crew was or where the Port was. After I had worked with my husband for fourteen years, this guy I had worked with in insurance called me and said, "We would love to talk to you and want to have you on board with us." It was a big company out of New York. They made me an offer. I wanted to try it for three months. By then, I had established knowledge of the marine industry and insurance is truly a necessity.

> But some of the men were just looking after me or looking out for me, so I could never say I had it so tough because I was a woman.

The coverage that we sell covers the crews of the vessels because they fall under an act called the Jones Act[1], instead of worker's compensation insurance. The coverage on a vessel is very similar to collision insurance on a car. They have huge deductibles—anywhere between $10,000 and $50,000, because the vessels are valued in the millions of dollars. Anytime there is an incident on the boat, it is pretty extensive or enough to get your attention. One of my friends had fourteen boats and one of his boats hit a fishing pier that had once been the bridge that connected Pensacola to Sea Breeze Island. When they built the big span across, instead of disassembling the bridge, they just left the pier, and part of it stuck out like a pier for people to use. They were coming through there and the wind caught them and shoved them into the pier. The water supply to the island was discontinued because it was damaged by the accident. We were all there for eight days. The news media was everywhere. The city manager, the mayor, everybody was down there. They saw that we were doing everything we could do to move the barge that was blocking their coastal region. We got it all taken care of and paid for. ∎

Interview conducted by Rebecca Marvil on December 19, 2013.
Photo by Loriana Espinel.

[1]The Merchant Marine Act of 1920, also known as the Jones Act, requires that all goods transported by water between U.S. ports be carried on U.S.-flag ships, constructed in the United States, owned by U.S. citizens, and crewed by U.S. citizens and U.S. permanent residents.

Old Boat, New Boat
Photo by Lou Vest

[TRANSFORMATIONS]

The early leadership of Houston, the so-called "city fathers," undertook a mighty and prolonged effort to fashion the city's bayous and Gulf Coast access into an unlikely and therefore unparalleled inland port. A combination of ingenious financing, haphazard land development, keen politics, over-the-top civic boosterism and natural disaster eventually led in 1914 to the realized dream of a commercial waterway linking the city to the rest of the country and connecting it with the entirety of the world. The development of the Houston Ship Channel was a stupendous achievement.

In the half-century following this achievement, the history of the Port was largely one of improvements in the waterway itself and the vessels it supported. During this period, the widening and deepening of the Channel facilitated modifications in the type and size of boats, barges and ships that could navigate it. Docks, terminals and warehouses were improved, expanded or built from the bottom up to answer the growing demand and the increasing traffic. Goods were loaded and unloaded, stored at and transferred to more sites by more people, but in much the same way in 1914 as they were until almost the 1960s. The amount of cargo increased but, with a few important exceptions, the types of materials imported and exported through the Port of Houston changed little.

In the past fifty years, however, the American workplace in general has been dramati- cally altered by mechanization, technology and pressing social issues. The Port of Houston and the Houston Ship Channel are no exception; in fact, they are an amazing demonstration of how these innovations have transformed the nature and quality of work in a particular occupational setting, have reduced the number of people and the time necessary to accomplish that work, and have reshaped the types of work available as well as the kind of knowledge these workers must deploy. Workers of all stripes, many still on the job today, have experienced a career-long process of adjusting to these developments—seeing progress and betterment for many in most of the changes, but also noting the loss of jobs and opportunity for others.

Simply put, all of the work of the Port is ultimately targeted toward the moving of materials of all kinds into and out of the Channel as efficiently as possible—loaded onto trucks or railcars to be transported from Houston to destinations near and far, or placed in and on ships and barges to be conveyed downstream or across the seas. This work of loading, placing and moving materials was forever altered by mechanization. Mechanization impacted the Port and Ship Channel workplace by shifting certain forms of manual and physical labor to machinery that could outwork the humanly possible. Cranes, derricks and forklifts were put to work to move not just a single item of cargo but an entire pallet. Piecework was replaced by cargo consolidated in containers and organized box on box.

Boatman of an earlier era.
Courtesy of Steve Bennett

Seafarers and longshoremen were the workers whose jobs absorbed the greatest impact. The first container ship that unloaded in Houston, in the mid-1950s, was a novelty, but containers utterly dominated the Port by the 60s. The sheer efficiency of moving a container directly from a ship to an eighteen-wheeler or a railcar meant that the size of the crew necessary to operate a ship or unload a hold, and the hours necessary for them to do so, diminished greatly. In explaining the importance of the International Seafarers Center, the late Father Rivers Patout spoke at length of the days when a ship would dock for a week and scores of sailors would spend time using the facility, swimming in its pool, playing soccer against other crews in its generous field.

The athletic program was very important in the early days—we had sports week and the winning ship got these big trophies and prizes and there was a dance and a big hoopla. So it was very active in the early days. We had one or two games every night. We have uniforms we'd give them. We even have shoes that were donated. Sometimes we had rivalry between the two ships; sometimes we bring a local team out to play. It was very active in the early days because they had time and they had people and they had **young** *people!*

Mark Henry, Boatman.
Photo by Lou Vest

With containerization and automation, though, these large crews were no longer necessary. Ships added equipment that made certain jobs obsolete and the gradual introduction of technology augmented this reduction in staff. Even tugs that worked the Channel cut back. Captain William Hennessey, who started on tugs in 1971, watched as this change transpired.

They [the ships] used to sail with a crew of thirty or more; now most ships are down to the low twenties. The tugs would have a crew of five to six, and would always carry a cook. Cooks were just no longer viable. Competition did away with them. Now some tugs operate with only two people on board. Those crews have definitely been reduced. Back then, if you had a boat running twenty-four hours a day, there would be a crew of four so that you would always have two people on watch. You would have one guy driving the boat, the captain or the mate and then you would have a deckhand on deck. Sometimes that could be a combination engineer. Now, they have combined some of the jobs, like you have "deck-ineers." That has reduced the number of people.

Though still an important institution, the Seafarers' Center now plays a far less social role than it did originally and its recreational facilities are seldom used. Sailors coming into the Port of Houston spend almost no time at dock and their needs are different. Patout compared the kind of activities that are increasingly important to a twenty-first century sailor and how they shape up against the kind of services they once provided and numbers they once assisted.

> *In the early days, it would be ordinary to have two hundred people a night up. I didn't have eleven people last night. Now, we do a lot of work. We provided the Wi-Fis, so they could use their computer on the ship. We provided telephones. We provided other aids to help them but the number of people coming in to the center—I think the biggest night we [had recently] was fifty-eight, because the church was putting on a party and they came to that. So that's a great night today.*

> *In the early days, that would have been a terrible night. The biggest change, of course, is the time in port and the number of people on a ship. When I started, forty was an average aboard a ship. Now twenty, if you're lucky, is an average aboard a ship. They'd be here a week—they get time to socialize, time to work, time to get their shopping done. Today, two days is a long time in port, and many would leave on the same day they come in.*

The Longshoremen's strike of 1968 was a direct result of these changes. Fear of job loss and reduced hours and wages in the face of containerization forced the International Longshoremen's Association (ILA) into a 108-day confrontation with management. All sides of this dispute describe the stand-off as devastating— to the workers and the industries whose products were stranded on the docks or in warehouses as well as to the businesses that played a supporting role in the work of the Port. Though the ILA garnered certain guaranties, those were not the most significant change. What the event did establish was that longshoremen, along with everyone employed along the Ship Channel, had to rethink the kind of future work for which they should prepare themselves. ILA official Andrew Laws explains the outcomes of this struggle:

> *The workforce is almost five times smaller than it was before, on account of automation and mechanization. The industry has changed from needing a strong back and a weak mind, to a strong mind and weak back. At one time, all you needed was to be was strong—to have the strength to pick up a sack and put it over here. Now you need some ingenuity; you need to be able to operate equipment that cost millions of dollars. Not everybody has the ability to operate those machines.*

Mechanization and automation made the workplace a more austere environment. Captain Hennessey remarks on just how significantly the landscape of the Port of Houston has changed. The Ship Channel industries of fifty years ago were operating on a smaller scale and were thus more informal in nature.

> *I started in the early 1970s, when you could drive in or walk in and out of any facility. It was much more relaxed and more enjoyable. That part has changed a lot. Now, when you are on a vessel, it is just like being in an office building.*

> *The biggest change is that everything got bigger. The harbor tugs are now three times the horsepower. Ships have become much bigger. It is not as much fun to work on these vessels. The ropes have gotten larger because the tugs are so much more powerful, but most of them are now on hydraulic or electric winches. So you can reel the line in and out just like it goes on a big fishing rod from the bridge. The need for extra people on the deck to do the heavy lifting is not there anymore.*

> *Everything is automated now in the engine rooms. So much of it is like operating a car: turn the key, start the engine, cast off the lines and go!*

Yet automation and its resulting efficiency have, paradoxically, put more responsibility on individual workers. As a result, training programs have become a far more significant aspect of entrée into participation in the Ship Channel workforce. For example, Gordie Keenan, Vice President for Training at Higman Marine, is quick to explain how important peer-to-peer sharing can be on the job; but he has also developed a rigorous training program for his employees. Instead of hiring to fill jobs, he is building a staff that will stay with the company. To do that, they must climb a very established education ladder. Just to progress beyond the entry-level position of deckhand and advance to tankerman, the process is elaborate and taxing. Keenan provides a quick overview:

> *At our company, there are four levels of tankermen. Each level gives them a higher pay grade. Some of them will want to go to the wheelhouse, which is the officers on the vessels that navigate the boat. It typically takes three years as a tankerman before starting the training for the wheelhouse positions. They need enough sea time, enough experience, and are required to be a tankerman at the higher levels. They then can apply for the steersman program. Steersman is the next level and is actually a training position. Steersman goes to school for three-and-a-half weeks and has to pass exams. Then they receive a steersman license from the United States Coast Guard which allows them to train on a towboat. That training*

takes about two years and they work under a licensed captain or mate. Throughout the process, they are tested by other captains in what we call "check rides" to ensure they are progressing. When they have enough sea time and have passed their check rides, application is made to the Coast Guard for the Mate of Towing license. This is the entry-level officer's license in the wheelhouse.

Containerization, automation and mechanization continue to inform and modify all of the jobs in the maritime world. But perhaps equally significant is the effect of electronic technology on the character of the work. Technology has had some impact on numbers of people employed in certain positions along the Ship Channel and, depending on the type of the technology, it can call for additional training that a standard worker might not have. Yet the greatest impact of electronic technology on the Port of Houston and the Houston Ship Channel is the speed at which information is now able to travel. Dave Morrell, one of the innovators behind a computerized monitoring program called Harbor Lights, recounts how this new technology has transformed the understanding of all activity occurring on the Ship Channel in real time.

Back in the old days, the Greater Houston Port Bureau oversaw the Marine Exchange. There was a beach home that was set up at Morgan's Point, which is the nearest part of the Channel. There were always some ladies out there—twenty-four hours a day, seven days a week, 365 days out of the year—with a pair of binoculars reading the names of the vessels

LEFT: Today programs like Harbor Lights help manage the Ship Channel, but ledgers like these would have been used before computer programs were available.
Courtesy of Steve Bennett
Photo by Brittney Gomez

RIGHT: Harbor Lights keeps everyone on the Channel in line and in the loop.
Courtesy of Harbor Lights

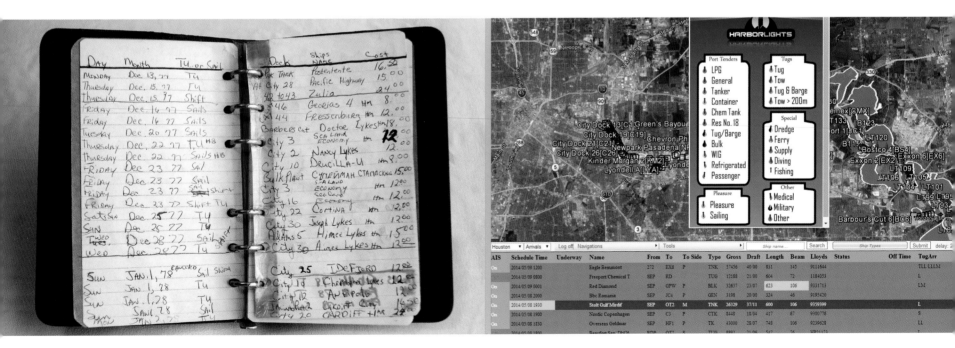

coming in and out. They would write them down, put the time down and save that information. It became report information for many people: ship agents, nautical lawyers, sheriff departments or the Port Authority itself.

By working with the Houston Pilots, who had developed a rudimentary system and who board and assist every ship that traverses the Channel, Morrell developed software to consolidate all of this information, including its requisites and restrictions.

With Harbor Lights, you can sit down and learn the system in a week or two. The ability is to make an accurate order without the experience that you had to acquire over the years. For example, when we first got in here, there was nothing on paper that said this was a rule or restriction. Everything was in everybody's head. Without getting that information from a pilot's head, dispatching was going to be impossible to do. There were little notes and there may have been books, but none of that was detailed.

Nowadays you make a quick assessment just by looking at the screen. The whole total data scheme is meant for the main scheduling services— the pilots, the tugs and the mooring companies. Information is restricted based on who you are, what level of security you have and what you are doing with the data. A pilot can access anything and everything.

Technology has sped up the transmission of information on the Houston Ship Channel to an almost revolutionary extent. Given the Port of Houston's specific characteristics and peculiarities, especially those having to do with the challenge of navigating a narrow, winding, comparatively shallow channel, the technical revolution has resulted in the ability to more effectively anticipate and maximize traffic on the Channel. Still, speed of information is important to more than just profitability and efficiency; it now plays a part in safety and response.

Environmental concerns are well served by the new technology: workers all along the Houston Ship Channel see speed as an initial, essential reaction. Rapid response is now the standard, as Admiralty Attorney James Patrick Cooney describes.

I have been to a lot of big spills. The last major oil spill I was involved with happened at eleven o'clock in the morning, and I was on the scene at two o'clock that afternoon. There is a rapid response function, a 24/7 response component to the business. Our job as maritime attorneys representing the spilling vessel initially is to make sure the response is being handled responsibly and that all the legal and regulatory requirements are being met. Then, as far as the response goes, it is our job to get out of the way and let the experts do their thing.

Indeed, the maritime industry has learned a great deal about response to environmental disasters and has been transformed in the process. Gordie Keenan, who has worked in a variety of occupations on the Houston Ship Channel, reflects on an incident that took place early in his career and how it has spurred momentous reforms.

> *The Valdez incident, besides being a bad ecological disaster, was probably the most important thing to happen to this industry worldwide and not just the U.S. It changed attitudes so much. It took an industry that was half-assed and turned it into the very professional, very incident, pollution conscious industry that it is today. If you look at the statistics of this industry, versus so many other industries, it is far beyond the other industries. The catalyst of that was the Valdez incident.*

Even Keenan's own professional decisions were profoundly influenced by the industry's strengthened commitment to the environment.

> *So would I still be in this industry if this Valdez event hadn't happened? I don't think so. To me, it wasn't very professional. Today it is a whole new different world. Our guys, on our boats, are managers. They are trying to do the best for the company and their customers.*

Just as the Exxon Valdez cataclysm brought dramatic changes to the shipping and petrochemical industries, a second event that unfolded far from Houston radically transformed the Port and the Ship Channel. On September 11, 2001, the attacks on the Pentagon, the Twin Towers in New York City and on United Airlines Flight 93 forced the United States government and its citizenry to recognize their vulnerability to outside antagonistic forces. In legitimate concern for the safety of its population and its essential infrastructure, the United States government mandated the closing of certain facilities to any but credentialed personnel. For the first time in almost ninety years, the Port of Houston and portions of the Houston Ship Channel, especially anywhere true work was done, became off-limits to the general public—to workers seeking jobs, to family members intent on visiting, to seafarers just arrived from a long voyage. The intent is understandable; the result deeply unfortunate, as Father Patout noted:

> *If you were a worker coming in, you have to have a TWIC [Transportation Worker Identification Credential] card. If you're a seafarer—American— you have to have one; now, foreigners can't own one. But even an American stationed right below our Center can look up there and see the Center, but he can't walk up to the Center anymore, unless somebody like myself with a TWIC and an escort card picks him up, brings him up and takes him back. So freedom of movement is horribly restricted. These are some of the real changes that have happened since 9/11.*

> *The worst possible thing that could have happened to seafarers is Homeland Security. The restrictions are so horrible—having to get visas in their own country before they're even allowed to consider getting off [the ship]—and they're very expensive visas. The restrictions when they get here—they're inspected ninety-six hours out to sea for any possible connection to terrorism. Then they're boarded by the Coast Guard and looked at and examined again when they're docked in. And when they're docked, Immigration goes again and checks each one of them. If they don't have the documentation, they cannot leave their ship. But even if they have the documentation, it's often the facility that makes it very difficult. We have people having to pay a couple hundred dollars to go a couple hundred yards from the ship to the gate, each way. You know, that's just horrible and an ordinary seafarer cannot afford that.*

Since 2010, when Patout offered these remarks, some of the most stringent restrictions have been amended. But it is still the case that the many young people who once found their way to, and possibly carved out a career from, the docks, shipyards, warehouses, factories and plants along the Ship Channel no longer can. Without a good deal of effort, parents cannot share their work directly with their children. Communities outside the hurricane fencing remain just that—outside.

Consequently, the Houston Ship Channel, an always under appreciated part of Houston city life has become more distant, obscured by precaution and restraint that is fully understandable, but antithetical to its true place in the local landscape. As the Port of Houston and the Houston Ship Channel have come to define so much of the region, they have also become more inscrutable, harder to characterize. Interestingly, it is the people themselves who work there—their stories and their experiences and their memories—that remind us of value of the Port. Their words of pride and persistence in the face of dramatic change, their spoken understandings of the ways the Port has woven itself into their lives: these are the most profound witnesses to its significance. ∎

WILLIAM HENNESSEY

EVERYTHING *got* BIGGER

OCCUPATIONAL OPPORTUNITIES AND CHOICES ARE OFTEN DEEPLY ROOTED IN FAMILY EXPECTATIONS, SOCIAL NETWORKS AND PRIDE. AT ITS OUTSET WILLIAM HENNESSEY'S STORY FITS A FAMILIAR PATTERN: A LONGTIME FAMILY OCCUPATION BEING PASSED ON TO HIM TO CARRY FORWARD INTO THE FUTURE. BUT THAT FUTURE TAKES SOME INTERESTING TWISTS AND TURNS AWAY FROM ITS STARTING POINT ON TUGBOATS THAT WORK THE WATERWAYS OF NEW YORK HARBOR. HENNESSEY'S LANDING IN BAYTOWN GIVES A GLINT OF THE GLOBAL SCALE OF MARITIME WORK IN THE TWENTY-FIRST CENTURY AND THE NEW OPPORTUNITIES THAT HOUSTON SHIP CHANNEL OFFERED HIM.

I was born in Brooklyn in 1951. My father was a tug captain, his father was a tug captain and that gave me an entrée into the business. Many of my relatives and friends were in the industry. I was in New York until 1971, when I started my first paid job in the tugboat industry with Texaco. They had a large tanker fleet and a lot of tugs back in the day. From there, I left Texaco in 1984 and went

to a company called Moran Towing, following closely in my father's footsteps—he was a pilot and tug captain and that was my destiny in life. That lasted until 1988 when there was a big tug strike in New York Harbor. In 1990, I got a call from Exxon to come work for them. So I went to work in 1990 in New York Harbor but quickly moved out to San Francisco.

We had a large operation in San Francisco Bay with Alaskan crude coming down to the Benicia refineries. So we had a number of tugs working in the bay and a number of the ships were constantly calling from Alaska to the port. In 2003, I got the call to see if I would be interested in taking up a shore assignment. That was after thirty years of being on harbor and ocean-going tugs, several voyages through the Panama Canal, East Coast, West Coast, Gulf Coast and Puerto Rico. We not only did the harbor work; we also did a lot of coastwise moving of product— petroleum product in barges.

I came to Houston in 2003 and have been on various assignments with quality assurance for vessels that were chartered all over the world. I went to the Middle East, Africa and Asia to get on board vessels to make sure they were up to the standards that we were looking for. About two-and-a-half years ago they transferred me to Baytown to fill the marine superintendent position at the refinery. I have been here two-and-a-half years and plan to stay a few more.

[
My father was a tug captain,
his father was a tug captain
]

HOUSTON HAS A UNIQUE KIND OF PORT—IT WAS ORIGINALLY LAND-LOCKED; A MAN-MADE SHIP CHANNEL WAS DREDGED AND CONTINUES TO POSE CHALLENGES TO MARITIME WORKERS ON THE SHIPS AS WELL AS SHORESIDE. THE NOW-RETIRED HENNESSEY NOTES THAT THE RESPONSIBILITY FOR DREDGING EXTENDS WELL BEYOND THE PORT OF HOUSTON AND TO PRIVATE SECTOR ENTITIES LIKE HIS FORMER EMPLOYER, EXXONMOBIL. AS MARINE SUPERINTENDENT, HE OVERSAW A VOLUME OF TRAFFIC AND SCALE OF OPERATIONS FOR THE CORPORATION THAT CLEARLY DEMONSTRATED ITS ROLE AS A MAJOR STAKEHOLDER.

The challenge in Houston is that we are always draft-constricted because of the silt. Over the course of a year, we accumulate sediment and lose depth. We dredge the berths because there's a lot of siltation coming in from the rivers that flow into the Channel. There is dredging in New York but nowhere near the amount of dredging that we have over here. There is no inland push boat traffic in San Francisco or in New York like the big inland tug and barge industry. So that is the big difference here, the inter coastal inland traffic in addition to ships and the deep-draft ocean barges.

We have an annual dredging project. I am responsible for working with the Port of Houston and the Army Corps of Engineers and contracting the dredgers that we use. A lot of permits are required once we make a decision to dredge. It takes about three months to start the process and it will take about three weeks to dredge all the docks here at Baytown so that we can maintain the same depth as the Ship Channel.

It is a very busy marine terminal, probably the busiest in the world for ExxonMobil. We have about 1800 barges that load or discharge from here and have about 500 ships a year that call at Baytown. It puts me pretty close to the maritime community without getting on a ship and sailing away. One of the primary responsibilities of a marine superintendent is assuring that the vessels that come to Baytown are acceptable. We have a vetting organization that makes sure the ships are up to a very high standard for charter. We make sure that ships fit on the berth. Houston is a forty-five-foot deep channel and we maintain a forty-five depth on our largest berths. So we make sure the vessel size and dimensions fit the assigned berth.

[
The challenge in Houston is that
we are always draft-constricted
because of the silt.
]

We also have safety advisors that go on board every ship and monitor the loading and discharging of the various products. There are a number of issues that come up with vessels. Most of the ships have inerted tanks and sometimes they have high oxygen levels in the cargo tanks, which could lead to delays or even reject the ship. We watch these operations very closely. That is something that I oversee; the safety advisors will visit every ship and barge that come to the facility.

EXXONMOBIL'S COMPLEX BAYTOWN FACILITY IS MASSIVE AND ITS PRODUCTIVITY IS STAGGERING. BUT AS HENNESSEY GOES ON TO EXPLAIN, SAFETY IS AN ESSENTIAL PART OF THE EQUATION THAT CANNOT BE SACRIFICED, DESPITE ITS IMPACT ON OPERATIONS,

LOGISTICS AND ECONOMIC EFFICIENCY. IT IS A DAUNTING PROCESS THAT MUST BE ENGINEERED AND MANAGED WITH PRECISION.

We have a limited number of refineries around the world. Baytown is the largest refinery in North America. We run about 580,000 crude barrels a day—ninety percent of that is waterborne, which means it comes in on ships. The rest comes in various pipelines. It is a very difficult business, very capital intensive, and it takes a lot of labor to keep it going. The Baytown Olefins Plant, Exxon Chemicals and the Baytown refinery make up the Baytown complex. It is a huge asset. We are seeing growth opportunities here, with a multibillion-dollar expansion planned for the complex. This is all good news. A lot of it is being driven by domestic production of crude and natural gas. It is all good news, not just for Baytown, but also for the Port of Houston and the entire region.

Safety is a priority, but we also have to be efficient with a limited amount of delays through various processes. Exxon prides itself on a safety record second to none. Fortunately, it has been many, many years since a big event on the dock. Nevertheless, a number of times a year, you are going to have a hard landing where the vessel will do damage to the dock and maybe do enough damage where we will have to take the dock out of service to be repaired. Each dock handles specific products, so that can be a challenge. We have a lot of people in the logistical chain; from the people that charter the ships and schedule them, to the allocators, to the refinery, to repair and maintenance people. We have contracts with people that come in and fix the problems, so there are a lot of logistics to manage. If there is an issue with somebody that gets hurt, we have a process in place to investigate and implement changes to make sure it doesn't happen again. We mitigate any risks as much as we can. In this industry, there is a policy of zero tolerance for accidents. So we want to engineer and manage the operations so they are done safely. Everybody can go home the same way they came to work. When you think of it in those terms it makes a lot of sense. That is basically what we want. There are a lot of safety meetings, lots of training; we take safety very seriously. Fortunately, the only incidents we have had during my time at Baytown have been very minor.

WITH MORE THAN FORTY YEARS UNDER HIS BELT, WORKING WIDELY THROUGHOUT THE MARITIME AND PETROCHEMICAL INDUSTRIES, HENNESSEY HAS A LONG AND BROAD VIEW OF THE CHANGES WROUGHT BY TIME.

The biggest change is that everything got bigger. The harbor tugs are now three times the horsepower. When I started, they were 1,600 horsepower; now there is an average of 6,000 horsepower. Ships have become much bigger. It is not as much fun to work on these vessels. The ropes have gotten larger because the tugs are so much more powerful, but most of them are now on hydraulic or electric winches. So you can reel the line in and out just like it goes on a big fishing rod from the bridge. The need for extra people on the deck to do the heavy lifting is not there anymore. Some of the heavy wires have been replaced by high module lines, which are very strong, stronger than steel, and lightweight.

> *The biggest change is that everything got bigger. The harbor tugs are now three times the horsepower.*

They used to sail with a crew of thirty or more, now most ships are down to the low twenties. The tugs would have a crew of five to six, and would always carry a cook. Cooks were just no longer viable. Competition did away with them. Now some tugs operate with only two people on board. Those crews have definitely been reduced. Back then, if you had a boat running twenty-four hours a day, there would be a crew of four so that you would always have two people on watch. You would have one guy driving the boat, the captain or the mate and then you would have a deckhand on deck. Sometimes that could be a combination engineer. Now, they have combined some of the jobs, like you have "deck-ineers." That has reduced the number of people.

[
*In this industry,
there is a policy of
zero tolerance for accidents.*
]

Everything is automated now in the engine rooms. So much of it is like operating a car: turn the key, start the engine, cast off the lines and go! If you were starting an engine years ago, only the engineer could do that. Now, you can push the button, start the engine and shut it down. Computers monitor everything, so if there is an issue with it you are going to get an alarm.

I started in the early 1970s, when you could drive in or walk in and out of any facility. It was much more relaxed and more enjoyable. That part has changed a lot. Now, when you are on a vessel, it is just like being in an office building. You have computers and phones and an enormous amount of documentation and paperwork to track. That has gone up by tenfold from when I started. A lot of changes were for the better. The quality management systems have been a huge benefit and have greatly reduced the number of injuries and accidents. It has made for much safer [work environments], a lot less pollution and that stuff is all good. The job has changed quite a bit, for the better mostly, but they do take a lot of fun out of it. ∎

Interview conducted by Pat Jasper on August 2, 2012.
Courtesy William Hennessey. Photo by Reverend David M. Rider.

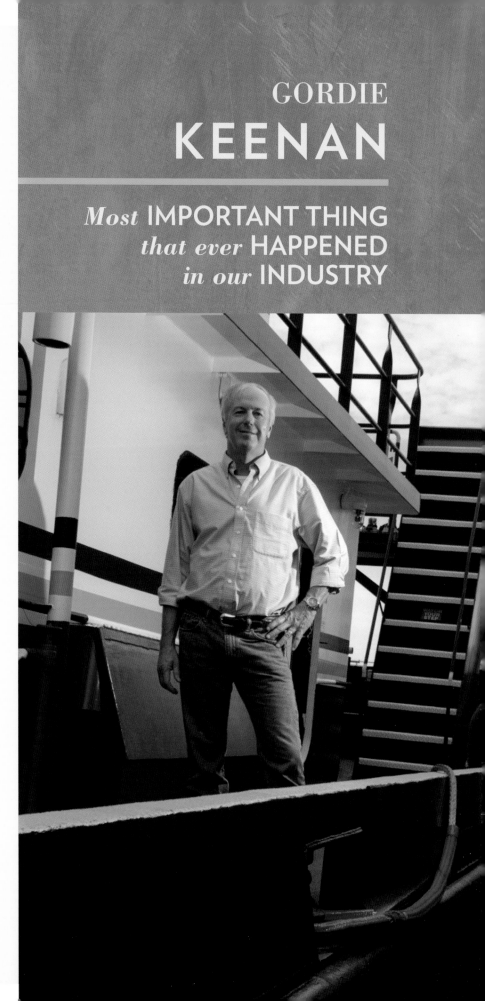

GORDIE
KEENAN

Most IMPORTANT THING
that ever HAPPENED
in our INDUSTRY

GORDIE KEENAN STARTED HIS CAREER AS THIRD ENGINEER ON AN EXXON OIL TANKER. IN 1977, HE WAS ONE OF THE FIRST FEW PEOPLE TO SAIL TO VALDEZ, ALASKA AS PART OF A CREW THAT TRANSPORTED CRUDE OIL FROM VALDEZ, ALASKA TO THE EXXON REFINERY IN CALIFORNIA. HE RECOUNTS HIS HISTORIC JOURNEY HERE.

I joined the shipping company Exxon after graduation as a third engineer on one of their oil tankers. It was a fortunate time in my life. Exxon would interview everyone and that was the job to get. I was one of the lucky guys to get selected by Exxon. They gave us an orientation down in Houston, and after three days, the guys from different academies were all together and they assigned us to the ships. I was assigned to the Exxon New Orleans. Its assignment was to sail south, go round Cape Horn, and go to Alaska, to Valdez. This was in June 1977 and our job was to load the first load of Alaskan crude via pipeline when it opened. So it was an historical trip for Exxon. These ships were too big to go through the Panama Canal. You have to go all the way around South America and it took us maybe fifty days to make it all the way around to Alaska. It turns out we were the second ship to load. A BP ship got there first. There was a ton of media. Valdez, at that time, was like a Wild West city. Streets were mud. There was no pavement. All these pipeline workers with plenty of cash were filling the bars—something out of the Wild West—drunk cowboys all over the place. We sailed in there, loaded the first load, all kinds of media was there. That was pretty exciting for me. We took the first load to San Francisco, California, where we discharged it at Exxon's refinery in Benicia.

OIL WELLS WERE DRILLED IN PRUDHOE BAY, ALASKA IN 1968, BUT IN 1977—AFTER BUILDING THE TRANS-ALASKA PIPELINE SYSTEM— OIL BECAME AVAILABLE AT VALDEZ FOR SHIPS TO TRANSPORT TO THE MAINLAND. ON MARCH 24, 1989, AN INCIDENT OCCURRED THAT ENSURED THE TOWN A PLACE IN THE HISTORY BOOKS: THE TANKER KNOWN AS THE EXXON VALDEZ STRUCK A REEF IN PRINCE WILLIAM SOUND. ITS HULL SPLIT OPEN AND DISCHARGED 11 MILLION GALLONS OF CRUDE OIL INTO THE ENVIRONMENT. AT THE TIME, IT WAS THE SINGLE BIGGEST SPILL IN US HISTORY. KEENAN TALKS ABOUT ITS DRASTIC IMPACT ON THE MARINE INDUSTRY.

The Valdez incident was probably, in my opinion, the most important thing that ever happened to our industry. Besides being a bad ecological disaster, it was probably the most important thing to happen to this industry worldwide and not just the U.S. It changed attitudes so much. It took an industry that was half-assed and turned it into the very professional, very incident-concerned, pollution-conscious industry that it is today. If you look at the statistics of this industry today, there have been significant changes for the good. The catalyst of that was the Valdez incident. So would I still be in this industry if this Valdez event hadn't happened? I don't think so. To me it wasn't very professional back then. Today it is a whole new world. Our guys, on our boats, are managers. They are trying to do the best for the company and their customers; back in the old days, they could get away with whatever you could.

> *Streets were mud. There was no pavement. All these pipeline workers with plenty of cash were filling the bars—something out of the Wild West— drunk cowboys all over the place.*

KEENAN TALKS ABOUT HIS COMPANY, HIGMAN MARINE SERVICES, THE WORK THEY DO AND THE TRAINING PROGRAMS HE OVERSEES. IT IS CLEAR THAT HIS URGE TO SEE THE FIELD PROFESSIONALIZE AND TO HELP CREATE A CONSCIENTIOUS WORKFORCE CONTINUES TO THIS DAY.

We are a towboat company. We have sixty towboats. Towboats are inland vessels. They don't go offshore. They are designed to work on rivers, bays and sounds, intracoastal waterways and canals. They are designed for that. They are a power unit that pushes barges. We own 120 barges and all are petroleum carriers. They are typically the same size—297 feet long and fifty-four feet wide. A typical boat will push two of those barges. So they have a 600-foot barge in front of them and they are typically between the barges that are carrying about 50,000 barrels of petroleum products from crude oil to six oil, from paraxylene to diesel, and all kinds of petroleum products that need to be moved for customers.

We have the boats and barges and people that work on them. They would start out as a deckhand, entry-level position. We bring them in, give them orientation and training. As far as credentials to get that job: they really don't need anything other than a TWIC card—a Transportation Worker Identification Credential. We hire them at this company, give them orientation, give them the clothes they need and assign them to a boat. The real training starts once they get on the boat. Tankermen is the next level that they need to get to in six to eight months. When they get to that level, we send them to tankermen school which is U.S. Coast Guard (USCG)-approved training. If they pass that training for five, six days, the Coast Guard will give them a PIC (Person In Charge) license. That allows them to load and discharge petroleum barges. Any barges that carry hydrocarbons.

At our company, there are four levels of tankermen. Each level gives them a higher pay grade. Some of them will want to go to the wheelhouse, which is the officers on the vessels that navigate the boat. It typically takes three years as a tankerman before starting the training for the wheelhouse positions. They need enough sea time, enough experience and are required to be a tankerman at the higher levels. They then can apply for the steersman program. Steersman is the next level and is actually a training position. Steersman goes to school for three-and-a-half weeks and have to pass exams. Then they receive a steersman license from the USCG, which allows them to train on a towboat. That training takes about two years and they work under a licensed captain or mate. Throughout the process, they are tested by oth-

er captains in what we call "check rides" to ensure they are progressing. When they have enough sea time and have passed their check rides, application is made to the Coast Guard for the Mate of Towing license. This is the entry-level officer's license in the wheelhouse.

On board one of our vessels typically are two tankermen, a steersman, a P, or pilot and the captain. The captain has a Master of Towing license which takes about three years of experience as a pilot. Pilot has the Mate of Towing license.

[*The real training starts once they get on the boat.*]

THE INDUSTRY ALSO TRIES TO BRING IN YOUNGER PEOPLE AND GROOM THEM INTO RESPONSIBLE AND DILIGENT MEMBERS OF THE MARITIME COMMUNITY. KEENAN TALKS ABOUT HOW ANYONE CAN APPLY FOR A BASIC LEVEL JOB AT HIS COMPANY, BUT ONLY THOSE THAT SHOW POTENTIAL TO GROW INTO P, OR PILOTS, AND CAPTAINS ARE ACCEPTED. HE ALSO UNDERSCORES THE AMOUNT OF LEARNING AND SKILL DEVELOPMENT THAT HAPPENS ON THE JOB, AS WORKERS AMASS EXPERIENCE AND COUNSEL AND ADVISE ONE ANOTHER.

Our hiring goal in the last few years has been hiring deckhands that have the potential to go into the wheelhouse and become managers and leaders on the boat. I find it very satisfying. It is kind of a hidden industry and sometimes hard to find people. It is a very different lifestyle too and we have to find the right person. So it takes a special person. We do hire from several different communities. We have a fair amount of family tradition. It is good so they understand what they are getting into. Most of the folks are from Texas, but some come from Mississippi, New Orleans and Mobile, Alabama.

There is a difference between deep-sea guys and pilots. It is because they have to use their senses and skills and intimate knowledge of the waterway to maneuver this big tow. You can have all the electronics in the world but to get around a bend with the current going in all different directions and you have to make a bridge. They learn through experience and through each other. We have a lot of technology, but it still goes back to the basic skills that go back to the Mark Twain days basically—understanding the rivers, understanding the canals, understanding how to line up a tow at a bridge. All these bridges are different depending on what the currents are doing, their flood and drought conditions. There is so much for these folks to learn and it is a lifelong process.

> We have a lot of technology, but it still goes back to the basic skills that go back to the Mark Twain days basically—understanding the rivers, understanding the canals, understanding how to line up a tow at a bridge.

A lot of the older guys will mentor. We do have computer-based training. We have seminars but the fundamental training is peer-to-peer. These guys learn from each other as they go along. That is so important in this business. We have older employees that have tons of experience that help us. We have several guys that no longer have licenses because of medical reasons. The Coast Guard is very strict on that. These experienced captains stay employed with us conducting check rides for steersmen and new hire P, or pilots. If we have a new P, or pilot, coming up, he has to be check rode by these experienced captains. So they will sign off on whether he is appropriate for that route.

IN ADDITION TO TRAINING, A HUGE PART OF REFORMING THE INDUSTRY LIES IN DEVELOPING TECHNOLOGY TO MEET THE DEMANDS OF THE CHANGING TIMES. KEENAN TALKS ABOUT HOW THE ONGOING REVOLUTION IN COMMUNICATIONS EACH AND EVERY BOAT IS NOW FITTED WITH THE LATEST TECHNOLOGY TO HELP THE CREW BECOME MORE INFORMED AND AWARE.

By far the biggest change has been in our communications. In the past, on the inland side, when I started in this business, you would call the boat on VHF radio through the marine operators. So the boats used to call the marine operators every morning on the VHF radio. They would give their position and if they had any repairs they needed, they would give that message at the time. But to get to the boat you had to figure out where the boat was, on what river, and call the local marine operators, and they would call on channel twenty-six, looking for the boat, and then you had to talk back and forth on the radio. That was how communication was; it was very difficult back in the '80s.

Today it is totally different. All our boats are outfitted with Internet. Through cell towers that are everywhere, there are very few places where there is no service. Our folks get their orders—they do all the forms they have to do. Everything including payroll is done on the wheelhouse computer. On board we do computer-based training programs. We have a learning management system that we use. That has been the biggest change—the ability to communicate with the boat. Now the cellular world has evolved so much you can do everything to cell. We have satellite capabilities in case of hurricane. ∎

Interview by Anthony Potoczniak on August 29, 2012.
Photo by Loriana Espinel.

DAVE
MORRELL

A *quick* ASSESSMENT JUST *by looking at* THE SCREEN

A CHALLENGE THAT HAS FACED THE HOUSTON SHIP CHAN-
NEL, FROM DAY ONE, IS ITS NAVIGATIONAL LIMITATIONS. ITS
DEPTH, WIDTH AND DRAUGHT WERE—AND REMAIN—SINGULARLY
SMALL, EVEN FOR AN INLAND PORT. THE GREAT LENGTH OF THE
CHANNEL CONTRIBUTED TO THESE TRIALS BY COMPOUNDING
COMMUNICATION DIFFICULTIES BETWEEN SHIPS AND AMONG THE
AREA'S INDUSTRIES AND ENTITIES. SOMETIMES JUST KNOWING
WHAT WAS AROUND THE BEND WAS AN IMPEDIMENT TO MOVE-
MENT AND EVEN A SOURCE OF STOPPAGE OR DELAY.

*Back in the old days, the Greater Houston Port Bureau
oversaw the Marine Exchange[1]. There was a beach home
that was set up at Morgan's Point, which is the nearest
part of the Channel. There were always some ladies
out there—twenty-four hours a day, seven days a week,
365 days out of the year—with a pair of binoculars read-*

[1] Under the Greater Houston Port Bureau, the Marine Exchange produces a daily Texas
ports movement report detailing arrivals and departures for the ports of Galveston,
Freeport, Texas City, Sabine, Port Comfort/ Lavaca, Corpus Christi and Brownsville.

ing the name of the vessels coming in and out. They would write them down, put the time down and save that information, and it became report information for many people: ship agents, nautical lawyers, sheriff departments or the Port Authority itself. The agent would have official notification that the vessel was here or that the vessel had left. A nautical lawyer or the sheriff's department or police department could be looking to physically serve papers on to the ship. So the information had value. It could also tell you how many times the ship had been in and out of the Port. The Marine Exchange never tracked vessels while they were in port. They just recorded if the ship ever came to port or not—whether it was coming in or leaving—like a headcount or ship count for the Port.

TO COMBAT THESE DIFFICULTIES, STRATEGIES WERE DEVELOPED FOR COMMUNICATING ESSENTIAL INFORMATION AMONG IMPORTANT PARTIES. DAVE MORRELL, A FOUNDER OF SOME OF THE MODERN TECHNOLOGY FOR DEALING WITH THESE PROBLEMS, REMEMBERS THE EARLIER APPROACHES AND TALKS ABOUT DEVELOPING A UNIQUE SCHEDULING SYSTEM THAT CHANGED ALL THAT. THE SYSTEM HE HELPED DEVELOP, HARBOR LIGHTS, ENDED UP ENHANCING ALL ASPECTS OF VESSEL MOVEMENT ON THE CHANNEL.

At some point, the Greater Houston Port Bureau began trying to record vessel information. I was already doing it for the Houston Pilots, and we were recording all that information. We started putting the information on the Internet for everyone, which meant not just the main scheduling services, but also the agents. It drove the beach house and the ladies with the binoculars out of business because there was no need for that anymore. The Marine Exchange persevered by putting together a product called MAPS, but we were already doing that here with the Houston Pilots system. It could deliver the exact same information more accurately than what MAPS was able to do. So it was just "jump in" and it was "sink or swim." They needed somebody with a computer background who could get this developed and that's what I did. It was just a really good union. They had a need; I had the ability to do it.

HOUSED IN THE SAME BUILDING, THE HOUSTON PILOTS AND THE HARBOR LIGHTS CREATED A COLLABORATION THAT IN TURN FACILITATED THE COLLABORATION BETWEEN THE PILOTS, WHO WERE PRIVY TO PARTICULAR KNOWLEDGE, AND THE DEVELOPERS, WHO BUILT A PRECISE SYSTEM THAT COULD BENEFIT A NUMBER OF BUSINESSES.

Harbor Lights is a scheduling system that uses pilot data [to dispatch ships]. The orders [to dispatch a ship] are made according to the dock's schedule from the Port Authority, but the vessel does not move until the pilot has boarded the ship and is ready to move the ship. The reason the scheduling system works effectively using pilot data is that the whole time the ship moves, the pilot is the only one that is with the ship 100 percent of the time.

Back when they started, the Houston Pilots had a database put together. It was good, but we were able to use it and expand into more things by adding more data into the system. Over time, we were able to automate a lot of the stuff. What we ended up doing was linking the Lloyd's database[2] to update the new vessels that have been verified by the pilots. Lloyd's can be off a few feet, a ton or two. So we developed our own accurate database using the pilot's information.

> [*It drove the beach house and the ladies with the binoculars out of business because there was no need for that anymore.*]

THE MUCH-TOUTED GROWTH AND UNPRECEDENTED INCREASE IN MARINE TRAFFIC ON THE CHANNEL HAS COMPLICATED AND SPEEDED UP VESSEL DISPATCHING, DOCKING, ARRIVALS, DEPARTURES AND MOVEMENTS. MORRELL'S EXPLANATION OF HARBOR LIGHTS DEMONSTRATES HOW TECHNOLOGY CAN AUTOMA-

[2] Lloyd's List is the leading daily newspaper for the maritime industry, covering all sectors of the shipping world including tankers, containers, ports and dry bulk.

TICALLY ENCODE ENORMOUS AMOUNTS OF INFORMATION THAT WAS ONCE THE RESPONSIBILITY OF INDIVIDUAL DISPATCHERS.

[An electronic] scheduling system could take the order without actually having to know the Channel, remember every restriction about that vessel, and where it's going. [In contrast,] it would take about three years to get a really good, seasoned dispatcher to dispatch a pilot or tug or whatever—it is not something you learn in a week, or a month, or a year. There is too much to know. With Harbor Lights, you can sit down and learn the system in a week or two. The ability is to make an accurate order without the experience that you had to acquire over the years. For example, when we first got in here, there was nothing on paper that said this was a rule or restriction. Everything was in everybody's head. Without getting that information from a pilot's head, dispatching was going to be impossible to do. There were little notes and there may have been books, but none of that was detailed.

[Nowadays,] you make a quick assessment just by looking at the screen. The whole total data scheme is meant for the main scheduling services—the pilots, the tugs and the mooring companies. Information is restricted based on who you are, what level of security you have and what you are doing with the data. A pilot can access anything and everything. So the pilots, tugs and moorings have all the information, which includes the dock notes and who is assigned to the ship. The rest of the industry is restricted from that information because it is not pertinent to their business.

HARBOR LIGHTS HEIGHTENED AND STANDARDIZED INFORMATION ABOUT MOVEMENT ALONG THE CHANNEL AND, IN SO DOING, COMPLETELY STREAMLINED THE WAY THE CHANNEL OPERATES. AND INEVITABLY, IT REORGANIZED WORK METHODS ACROSS MANY PORT OCCUPATIONS.

It is like trickle-down economics. You take the information from the first service that starts the order (the pilots), and filter that out to the other services that have the information, and keep it up to date as it changes. That's what made it very effective. Throughout the years, it has helped optimize the Port, not only in how many ships it can move, but also in terms of security because it keeps more eyes on the vessel. It is the only scheduling system service within the Port that stays with the vessel for the complete time that it is here.

[
It is not something you learn in a week, or a month, or a year. There is too much to know
]

Before, with the older dispatchers—whether it was a pilot or tug, mooring company, lineman—they all had a system. It was usually a piece of paper that they wrote on or kept notes, or it might go in a spreadsheet. They don't have to use that system anymore; they can just use the Harbor Lights screen. The methods that were used in the old days are not passed along to the new people that come around. The Harbor Lights system is what they are used to using, so it has become a staple for the major scheduling companies. There is no other tool available when the old methods have gone. It has made a change in the way things are done. ▮

Interview conducted by Anthony Potoczniak on July 31, 2012.
Photo by Jack Potts.

DANA
BLUME

PEOPLE, *Planet*, PROFIT

PORTS AND THEIR SURROUNDING COMMUNITIES ARE DEFINED BY THE TRANSPORT OF A WIDE RANGE OF MATERIALS BY NUMEROUS TYPES OF VEHICLES. THAT MEANS THAT ITEMS LIKE PETROCHEMICALS, GRAINS, CARS AND MANUFACTURED GOODS ARE BEING MOVED BY SHIPS, TRAINS AND TRUCKS. THE PRESENCE OF THIS COMBINATION IN A COMMUNITY CAN HAVE LONG-LASTING EFFECTS ON THE QUALITY OF LOCAL AIR, WATER AND SOIL. WHILE THE INTERESTS OF INDUSTRY AND THE ENVIRONMENT CAN OFTEN BE AT ODDS, THERE ARE THOSE WHO WORK TO BALANCE THE ECONOMIC, COMMUNITY AND ENVIRONMENTAL IMPACTS OF INDUSTRIAL ENTERPRISE. DANA BLUME OF THE PORT OF HOUSTON AUTHORITY (PHA) DISCUSSES ITS ROLE IN ENVIRONMENTAL OVERSIGHT.

I came to the Houston Port Authority in 1999. In the fourteen years that I have been here, I can say that the environmental attitude has definitely changed for the better. There are the three Ps—people, planet and profit. While we all do things to make money, the planet should be a number one focus. I have a passion for air quality and making sure that the operations at the Port Authority and its tenants are as clean as we can get them. That has been my big focus for the past fourteen years.

BEFORE SHE JOINED THE AUTHORITY, BLUME WORKED WITH AN OIL COMPANY ON A PROJECT THAT RESHAPED HOW SHE VIEWED THE RELATIONSHIP BETWEEN INDUSTRY AND COMMUNITY.

I participated in one of the largest pipeline-decommissioning projects in North America called the Pony Express Pipeline. An old Amoco crude oil pipeline had been purchased by a company called KN Energy, and was going to be converted into a natural gas pipeline. It was almost a thousand miles long and it went through five states. I worked on that project for a solid two-and-a-half years of my life, but it really gave me a deep appreciation for how sensitive the environment is in every little thing that we do. We were testing an old pipeline that was not necessarily welded for that application, so it ruptured a lot and we had to go in and perform clean-up activities. It gave me more of a people side to the environmental—it was not just about how we would impact the soil, water or the wetlands—we were also coming on people's property and impacting it—replacing it and trying to make it better.

That was always something that I liked. Wherever we went, we always tried to leave it nicer than it was to begin with. Sometimes it meant they got a new fence or a nice roadway that was paved. That is something oil companies do a lot. I appreciated that. I appreciated the emergency response part of it too. Most of the time, when there is a rupture, it was not in an easy spot to get to. You have to concentrate, not just on the environment, but also how it is going to impact the citizens or the community in that area. Are they going to worry about what is or going to get into the water or the air in the area and how it is going to impact the economy? Is it going to shut something down? Sometimes, a spill stimulates the economy because a lot of local folks get involved and help with clean-up efforts. The Pony Express Pipeline project really practiced sustainability in all three aspects—people, planet and profit. I have learned that what I was doing at the pipeline project is what I have carried over here to the Port of Houston Authority.

> [*While we all do things to make money, the planet should be a number one focus.*]

A CENTRAL ISSUE FOR BLUME AND HER CURRENT EMPLOYER IS "STEWARDSHIP." AS BLUME EXPLAINS, STEWARDSHIP ENTAILS BOTH COMPLIANCE ISSUES—WHICH INCLUDE OBSERVING ENVIRONMENTAL REGULATIONS—AND VOLUNTARY ACTIVITIES, WHICH SHE AND THE PHA PERFORM TO PROTECT AND CONSERVE THE NATURAL WORLD THAT SURROUNDS THE SHIP CHANNEL.

We are right on the water, so the Port Authority also takes care of water quality issues, from storm water to drinking water and all the permitting issues in between. We stay up-to-date on national programs, legislation and regulations. Following the Clean Water Act[1] is a big deal—it impacts us all. One neat thing about the Port of Houston Authority is that we are a dual-role port; we are a landlord, as we lease out property to others, but we are also an operating port. Not a lot of ports have dual roles. We would not ask or expect a tenant to do anything that we are not doing ourselves, especially when it is compliance driven.

We expect everyone to be completely compliant with federal and state rules and regulations, but when it comes to the stewardship programs, which are primarily what the air quality program has been about, we try everything out first. Whether it is a new widget to put on that engine to see whether it reduces emissions, or a new fuel, or a new operating policy or procedure—such as no idling—we do it first. We find out if it works or doesn't and then share it with everyone. That attitude has helped the air quality program be one of the leading programs in the country, especially from the environmental sustainability perspective where we try to keep in balance the economics of it, as well as the community impacts.

In terms of stewardship, we look at the environmental department and all of its programs in two realms—compliance driven and stewardship based. Water quality is one hundred percent compliance driven. It has permits and deadlines and audits and inspections. The air quality program, in my opinion, is mostly a stewardship program. According to the Clean Air Act[2], our area has to meet a certain attainment criteria for ozone. You can have good and bad ozone. We need all of it, but too much of something is a bad thing. Our area [Houston] is nonattainment for ozone and close to nonattainment for particulate matter, which can be the dust and soot material coming from an unpaved property or out of an exhaust pipe or even a stack[3].

BUT, AS BLUME REPORTS, THERE ARE MANY "PLAYERS" ALONG THE SHIP CHANNEL AND ANY ACCIDENT, INCIDENT, VIOLATION OR DISTURBANCE MAY INVOLVE MANY PARTIES.

[1]The comprehensive federal law that establishes the basic structure for regulating discharges of pollutants into the waters of the United States and regulating quality standards for surface waters. Enacted in 1948, but amended in 1972 to its more commonly known state.

[2]The comprehensive federal law enacted in 1970 that regulates air emissions from stationary and mobile sources.

[3]According to the EPA (Environmental Protection Agency), if the concentration of one or more criteria pollutants in a geographic area is found to exceed the regulated or threshold level for one or more of the NAAQS (National Ambient Air Quality Standards), the area may be classified as a nonattainment area.

Today, we don't have a big contamination problem, per se, along the Houston Ship Channel, like one would think we would since the Ship Channel is home of the largest petrochemical complex in the nation. The Ship Channel is a very heavily regulated industry, from an air, water and waste perspective. So, what they are discharging is not a free-for-all. They have to submit reports and they are routinely inspected. So, for the most part, our sediment is clean. There are some bad players, whether they are intentionally or they don't know it. For example, we have had contamination in Greens Bayou where it was impacted by DDT[4]. The state regulators knew about it, and the company that was impacting it knew about it, but we couldn't get anyone to clean it up until we actually filed a lawsuit against the company. It was settled out of court and about ten years later, it is finally cleaned up. The contamination on Greens Bayou really highlighted the importance of our sediment management guidelines.

BLUME ALSO CONSIDERS A CRUCIAL, BUT PERHAPS LESSER-KNOWN PRACTICE THAT MAINTAINS THE PORT IN WORKING ORDER—THE DREDGING AND SUSTAINABLE MANAGEMENT OF SEDIMENT, WHICH HAS AN IMPACT ON COASTAL ENVIRONMENTS IN GENERAL[5].

It is important to keep the Channel as deeply dredged as it can be or at the permitted level. For example, if the Port is supposed to be forty or forty-five feet and you can only gets a ship in that draughts 40 feet, that is 5 feet of draught depth that you are not able to get on that ship, which means it has to bring less cargo in. Two things can happen. The ship could decide to go somewhere else with fewer restrictions or the ship brings less cargo in, which can mean either more ships, which also means more air emissions, or just less cargo overall, which means less for you in the store to purchase or consume.

Along the Houston Ship Channel, there are different areas with big spots of land. You may think, "Why isn't PHA developing those areas?" Most of those areas are dredge placement areas, or what we call confined disposal facili-

ties. The Houston Ship Channel and Port Authority have done two things. One, we use dredge material to build up areas and put them into dredge placement areas. In the future, when that area is no longer used, it could be developed into property for operations. Second, the Port, along with various partners and stakeholders, has developed programs to use dredge material and create marshes.

WITHOUT DREDGING THERE WOULD BE NO PORT OF HOUSTON, AS WE KNOW IT TODAY. DREDGING WAS KEY TO CREATING THE ORIGINAL INLAND PORT AND IT REMAINS EQUALLY CRUCIAL TO KEEPING THE CHANNEL FULLY NAVIGABLE. HOWEVER, THE PROCESS CAN DISTURB AN ECOSYSTEM AND SPREAD UNNECESSARY SILT IN THE WATER, BUT BLUME NOTES ALTERNATIVE USES OF THE MATERIALS DREDGED AS A FORM OF MITIGATION THAT HAS PRODUCED SURPRISING OUTCOMES.

Now the Houston Ship Channel is basically man-made, but it was originally a small, meandering little bayou. All the bayous in Houston flow into it. Almost one hundred years ago, Houston visionaries thought to dredge it up and have a channel where ships can come and go, but today, it remains a big task to keep it dredged. A lot of that material is sand and silt, and some of it is hardpan clay. They have utilized this clay to make demonstration marshes and have cut small channels into the marshes where individuals can kayak. These placement areas also become habitats for bird rookeries. So we have created or planned to create around 4,200 acres of marsh area, with material that would have otherwise gone into a placement area or a landfill. The Port Authority recognizes that the material is so good, we could utilize it to create other things, such as destination points for boaters or scientists to do research. I am proud that we not only implement the standards that EPA and the U.S. Army Corps of Engineers have put in place, but we manage to go even beyond and be better. ∎

Interview conducted by Pat Jasper on August 6, 2012.
Photo by Lou Vest.

---

[4]DDT is a poisonous chemical that was used as an insecticide and is now banned in the U.S.
[5]According to the Coastal Sediment Workgroup, sediment is an integral component of the coastal ecosystem, representing a public good that must be managed to provide for quality of life, natural resource protection, and economic sustainability. Sediment imbalances resulting from alteration of the natural environment therefore threaten the viability of the public good and require management to restore the natural balance.

[ACKNOWLEDGEMENTS]

My greatest thanks with regard to this publication and this project goes to the city of Houston. How unlikely for me, a long time Central Texan, to wake up one day in love with a city as complex and challenging as Houston. I wondered at it then. I wonder at it now.

In 2010, my unfiltered sense of the city extended to the remarkable personal realization of how vital the Port of Houston and the Houston Ship Channel are to the area. I would travel to Brady's Island to watch the massive ships come in. I would marvel at their vastness and the amazing pallet of colors that these vessels of steel would sport. I would drive, and turn around and re-redrive, the Loop 610 Bridge over the Channel, staring at the vast lots of newly imported cars. I would hang out in Hidalgo Park staring downstream. I would ride the Lynchberg Ferry and the Sam Houston Tour Boat. As I blasted southeast on Highway 225 I would gawk at the warehouses and the tanks and the towering flares shooting into the sky. I would stand at the Santa Ana capture site, over the Washburn tunnel, and listen to the sounds of the channel and get as close to the water as anyone could these days. I would go to meetings where I knew no one and everyone seemed to know each other. I was transfixed by what was the mostly impenetrable world of the Port.

Like much of Houston, the Ship Channel doesn't mess around; it's all business, and there is little or no posturing. Boosterism in Port terms is all tonnage and ratings and TEUs and economic multipliers; not average days of sunshine, or great places for excellent views, or interesting excursions for the adventuresome. The neighborhoods that surround it are modest and the businesses betray a kind of make-do character —maritime machinery this decade and petrochemical gauges and gewgaws next. The ethos is strictly work and work is what the Port is about. But that work really has a life and that life is the tens of thousands of people who occupy the jobs that make the Port run in all its enormity and complexity. And, in a sense, therein lies its anonymity, its invisibility, its inscrutability.

So, with that said, I must begin by acknowledging all of those workers who shared their words and their worlds with me. I am grateful to all who, by their generous expense of time and their candid recounting of their stories, drew a picture for me, taught me things I never imagined I'd know, shared personal insights and historic moments. My welcome from the beginning came from individuals who understood the importance of what I might be trying to do—Walt Neimand, retired from West Gulf Maritime Association, Father Rivers Patout of the Tellepson Seafarers Center, Captains Ted Thorjussen and James

Baker. At some point I met a number of people from the International Longshoremen's District office, like Benny Holland and Andrew Laws. Somehow, I tripped over Houston Pilot and world class photographer Lou Vest. These were all people who understood why the personal stories of their work and their colleagues' work were important to document. It was these individuals who made it possible.

The institutions that made a difference are less predictable and, honestly, somewhat unexpected. Much to my amazement, my boss and the CEO of the Houston Arts Alliance, Jonathon Glus, loved the idea of this project. My colleagues at the American Folklife Center at the Library of Congress comprehended the project's value so fully that they awarded me an Archie Green Fellowship to launch the Working the Port project, which allowed me to conduct the interviews. Raj Mankad of CITE magazine, published by the Rice Design Alliance, pursued me and my colleague, Dr. Carl Lindahl, for the first public manifestation of this project. The Summer 2012 issue featured a special focus on the Port and featured the Father Rivers Patout and Lou Vest interview excerpts contained here. This outing gave interested individuals a sense of the project's potential. Another institution that has assisted greatly is the Houston Public Library, especially Director Dr. Rhea Lawson, curator Danielle Burns and her associate Christina Grubitz.

In regard to undertaking both the Working the Port project and transforming it into the exhibition *Stories of a Workforce: Celebrating the Centennial of the Houston Ship Channel*, I have many to thank for the direct and significant involvement. My fellow folklorists, Betsy Peterson (now at the Library of Congress) and Carl Lindahl, of the University of Houston, joined forces to assist immediately. Along the way, David Theis, Anthony Potozniack, Rebecca Marvil and Harold Dodd contributed interviews. Linda Ho Peche, Rati Ramadas Girish and Harold Dodd assisted with excerpting and framing the interview selections included here. Rati Ramadas Girish and Angel Quesada did most of the processing and logging and transcribing. Angel Quesada, Danielle Burns, Christina Grubitz, Gabriella Flournoy, Rati Ramadas Girish and Rebecca Marvil have worked on various aspects of the exhibit. HAA colleagues for which I have much thanks include development Director Kate Ostrow Yadan and Communications Director Marie Jacinto. And, last but by no means least, every person who granted an interview has played a very central role in the project and in all that has gone into the exhibition. They are all named at the back of the catalog.

–Pat Jasper

[GLOSSARY OF TERMS]

AFT: Towards or at the back part of a boat.

ADMIRALTY LAWYER/ATTORNEY: One who practices law which pertains to the sea.

(U.S.) ARMY CORPS OF ENGINEERS: A U.S. federal agency which seeks to deliver vital public and military engineering services, strengthen security, energize the economy and reduce risks from disasters.

BARGE: A flat-bottomed boat for carrying freight, typically on canals and rivers, either under its own power or towed by another.

BEAM: The width of a ship.

BITTS: A pair of vertical wooden or iron posts on the deck of a ship, used to secure mooring or towing lines.

BOATMAN: A mariner who earns a living by transporting people or cargo by boat.

BOATSWAIN: The highest unlicensed rating in the deck department who has immediate charge of all deck hands and who in turn comes under the direct orders of the master or chief mate or mate.

BOW THRUSTER: A propeller at the bow of the ship which increases maneuverability in confined areas, especially when docking.

BREAK BULK CARGO: Goods loaded individually into the hold of a ship and not put in uniform shipping containers.

BREAK BULK VESSEL: A general, multipurpose, cargo ship that carries cargoes of non-uniform sizes, often on pallets, resulting in labor-intensive loading and unloading.

CONTAINER: A reusable steel box designed for storing and transporting goods. They are measured in twenty-foot equivalent units (TEU), an inexact unit used to describe the capacity of container ships and terminals. The most common container size is forty-feet long, or two TEU.

DRAFT: The depth of a ship in the water, measured from the bottom of the ship to the waterline.

GUARANTEED ANNUAL INCOME: A payment program started in 1964 by the International Longshoreman's Association to offset the loss of wages and jobs from containerization.

INTERNATIONAL LONGSHOREMEN'S ASSOCIATION (ILA): The largest union of maritime workers in North America, representing upwards of 65,000 longshoremen on the Atlantic and Gulf Coasts, Great Lakes, major U.S. rivers, Puerto Rico and Eastern Canada.

INTERNATIONAL LONGSHORE & WAREHOUSE UNION (ILWU): The labor union which primarily represents dock workers on the West Coast of the United States, Hawaii and Alaska, and in British Columbia, Canada.

KNOT: Unit of speed equal to one nautical mile per hour (6,076 feet per hour)

LINE HANDLER: A person who secures a boat or ship to the dock.

LONGSHOREMAN: A laborer who loads and unloads cargo onto ships. See also Stevedore.

MARINE EXCHANGE: An organization which seeks to collect, analyze and disseminate ship traffic information.

MASTER OF TOWING: A license required to be the first or second captain on tugboats and towing vessels.

MERCHANT MARINE (OR MERCHANT NAVY): The fleet of U.S. civilian-owned merchant vessels, operated by either the government or the private sector, that engage in commerce or transportation of goods and services in and out of the navigable waters of the United States.

MONKEY FIST: A type of knot, so named because it looks somewhat like a small bunched paw. It is tied at the end of a rope to serve as a weight, making it easier to throw.

PACIFIC MARITIME ASSOCIATION: An organization whose mission is to negotiate and administer labor agreements with the International Longshore and Warehouse Union.

PERSON IN CHARGE (PIC): An endorsement earned after special training, usually held by someone in charge of transferring fuel oil to and from a vessel.

RO-RO (ROLL-ON/ROLL-OFF) RAMP: Used to maneuver vehicles on and off freight ships.

RO-RO (ROLL-ON/ROLL-OFF) SHIP: Freight ship with openings equipped with built-in ramps at the bow or stern for vehicles to drive on and off.

STEERSMAN: A person who steers a boat or ship.

STEVEDORE: Laborer employed in ship cargo handling. See also Longshoreman.

SWAMPER: Occupational slang for an assistant worker, helper, maintenance man or a person who performs odd jobs.

TANKERMAN: A person who works aboard a vessel involved in the transfer of liquid cargo from ships to tankers or barges.

TEUs: An abbreviation for the size of containers utilized on ships, railcars and 18-wheeler trucks—the Twenty foot Equivalent Unit.

TRANSPORTATION WORKER IDENTIFICATION CREDENTIAL (TWIC): A tamper-resistant biometric card given to maritime workers requiring unescorted access to secure areas of port facilities, outer continental shelf facilities, and vessels regulated under the Maritime Transportation Security Act of 2002.

TUG: A boat that maneuvers vessels by pushing or towing them.

VESSEL TRAFFIC SERVICE (VTS): A marine traffic monitoring system established by harbor or port authorities, similar to air traffic control for aircraft.

WALKING (GANG) FOREMAN: An experienced worker who has the authority to supervise, regulate work, place or discharge longshore workers.

WEST GULF MARITIME ASSOCIATION (WGMA): An organization which negotiates and administers various multiemployer collective bargaining agreements with the International Longshoremen's Association in West Gulf ports.

WHEELHOUSE: A room or compartment located on the highest deck, from which a captain or pilot can control or navigate the ship.

WINCH: A mechanical device used for hoisting or lowering heavy loads.

WINCHMAN: A worker who moves heavy objects by means of a winch.

[INTERVIEW LIST]

Niels Aalund, *Pat Jasper*	3/19/2012	
Douglas Adkinson, *Linda Ho Peche*	10/8/2013	
Captain Bains, *Harold Dodd*	3/23/2013	
Pat Bellamy, *Linda Ho Peche*	10/8/2013	
Steven Bennett, *Pat Jasper*	1/12/2012	
Richard Bludworth, *Pat Jasper*	1/6/2012	
Dana Blume, *Pat Jasper*	8/6/2012	
Leo Braun, *Elizabeth Peterson*	1/10/2012	
Joe Burkett, *Pat Jasper*	3/8/2012	
Van Chatman, *Rebecca Marvil*	4/11/2014	
James Patrick Cooney, *Pat Jasper*	2/24/2012	
Holly Cooper, *Rebecca Marvil*	5/19/2014	
Dean Corgey, *Pat Jasper*	2/21/2012	
Michael Cordua, *Linda Ho Peche*	10/21/2013	
Carlos de Aldecoa Bueno, *Rebecca Marvil*	4/15/2014	
William Diehl, *Pat Jasper*	3/15/2012	
Michael Dickens, *Elizabeth Peterson*	11/15/2011	
Clyde Fitzgerald, *Elizabeth Peterson*	9/9/2011	
Sonny Flores, *David Theis*	7/11/2012	
Charles H. Gage, *Pat Jasper*	9/8/2011	
Matthew Hance Glass, *Harold Dodd*	9/12/2012	
Robert Leonard Glass, *Harold Dodd*	8/21/2012	
Homer Guillory, *Pat Jasper*	4/19/2014	
David Halbert, *Pat Jasper*	2/28/2012	
William Hausinger Jr., *Elizabeth Peterson*	10/20/2011	
Eugene Harris, *Elizabeth Peterson*	11/15/2011	
T.C. Harris, *Elizabeth Peterson*	11/16/2011	
Deltrick Harrison, *David Theis*	10/23/2012	
William Hennessey, *Pat Jasper*	8/2/2012	
Mark Henry, *Pat Jasper*	10/30/2012	
James J. Hensley, *Elizabeth Peterson*	10/20/2011	
Henry Hillard, *Pat Jasper*	10/26/2012	
Townsend Hillard, *Pat Jasper*	10/26/2012	
Benny Holland, *Pat Jasper*	9/9/2011	
Gordie Keenan, *Anthony Potoczniak*	8/29/2012	
Bobby Kersey, *Elizabeth Peterson*	10/11/2011	
Joseph Kinch, *Pat Jasper*	4/19/2014	
Charles King, *Elizabeth Peterson*	1/11/2012	
Vidal Knight, *Rebecca Marvil*	12/19/2013	
George Larrimer, *Anthony Potoczniak*	8/1/2012	
Andrew Laws, *Pat Jasper*	9/8/2011	
Lindberg Lebert, *Elizabeth Peterson*	10/20/2011	
Captain Tom Lightsey, *Pat Jasper*	9/27/2011	
Gilbert Martinez, *Harold Dodd*	9/26/2011	
Donnie D. Mayville, *Harold Dodd*	10/4/2012	
Victor Medina, *David Theis*	11/6/2013	
Frank Merrill, *Linda Ho Peche*	3/12/2014	
Doug Mims, *Anthony Potoczniak*	9/3/2012	
Charles Montgomery, *Elizabeth Peterson*	9/7/2011	
Dave Morrell, *Anthony Potoczniak*	7/31/2012	
Walt Neimand, *Elizabeth Peterson*	1/11/2012	
Eric Olsen, *Pat Jasper*	/23/2012	
Schway Tan Ong, *David Theis*	7/27/2012	
Father Rivers Patout, *Pat Jasper*	7/26/2010	
William Benjamin Patton Jr., *Pat Jasper*	3/1/2012	
Charlie Lou Paysse, *Elizabeth Peterson*	9/8/2011	
George Peterkin, Jr, *Rebecca Marvil*	4/10/2014	
Adolph Postel Sr., *Pat Jasper*	2/27/2011	
Gilda Ramirez, *Pat Jasper*	6/8/2012	
Alan A. Robb, *Elizabeth Peterson*	11/15/2011	
David A. Rodriguez, *Pat Jasper*	4/27/2014	
C.A. Rousser, *Pat Jasper*	11/15/2011	
Harold Schaffer, *Elizabeth Peterson*	9/8/2011	
Patrick Seeba, *Anthony Potoczniak*	7/19/2012	
Pat Studdart, *Pat Jasper*	4/27/2012	
Tom Tellepsen II, *Pat Jasper*	3/29/2012	
Terry Thibodeaux, *Pat Jasper*	11/14/2010	
Robert Thompson, *Harold Dodd*	9/10/2012	
James Thomas Tray, *Pat Jasper*	3/2/2012	
Michael Gene Usher, *Pat Jasper*	7/16/2012	
Lou Vest, *Carl Lindahl*	11/8/2011	
Fred Warner, *Pat Jasper*	4/26/2012	
John Ray Whaley, *Linda Ho Peche*	10/8/2013	

[BIBLIOGRAPHY:]

Falloure, David H. *Sheer Will; The Story of the Port of Houston and The Houston Ship Channel.* San Bernardino: CreateSpace Independent Platform, 2014. Print.

Falloure, David. *Houston Ship Channel: Open to the World.* Houston, 2014. Print.

Flynn, Andrea K. *Tom Tellepsen, Builder & Believer; a Biography.* Salado, TX: Anson Jones, 1956. Print.

George, Rose. *Ninety Percent of Everything: Inside Shipping, the Invisible Industry That Puts Clothes on Your Back, Gas in Your Car, and Food on Your Plate.* New York: Metropolitan / Henry Holt, 2013. Print.

Kreneck, Thomas H. *Del Pueblo: A History of Houston's Hispanic Community.* College Station: Texas A&M UP, 2012. Print.

Mers, Gilbert. *Working the Waterfront: The Ups and Downs of a Rebel Longshoreman.* Austin: U of Texas, 1988. Print.

Sibley, Marilyn McAdams. *The Port of Houston: A History.* Austin: U of Texas, 1968. Print.

Vela, Lee, and Maxine Edward. *Reaching for the Sea: The Story of the Port of Houston.* Houston, TX: Port of Houston Authority, 1989. Print.

[BOOKS]

Marguerite Johnston, *Houston, The Unknown City, 1836–1946* (College Station: Texas A&M University Press, 1991).

David G. McComb, *Houston, a History* (Austin: University of Texas Press, 1981).

Marilyn M. Sibley, *The Port of Houston* (Austin: University of Texas Press, 1968).

[ONLINE RESOURCES]

http://www.portofhouston.com/about-us/history/

http://www.portofhouston.com/about-us/overview/

http://www.portofhouston.com/static/gen/inside_the_port/Communications/ Factsheets/port_of_houston_first.doc

http://www.tshaonline.org/handbook/online/articles/rhh11

https://www.worldportsource.com/ports/review/USA_TX_Port_of_Houston_60.php

[GUIDES AND HANDOUTS]

World Affairs Council of Houston and Houston Arts Alliance, *Celebrating 100 Years of The Port of Houston: An Educator's Guide.* Chapter 7: History of the Port of Houston and the Ship Channel, pp. 141-151.

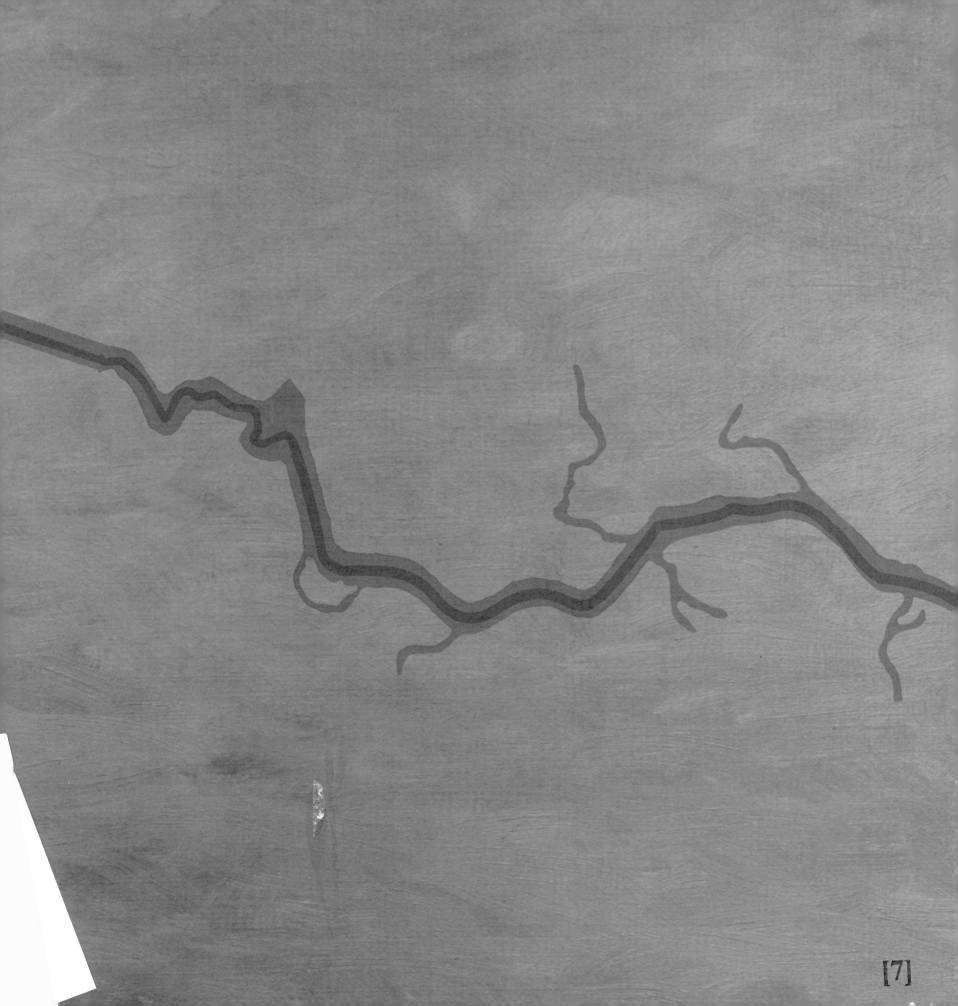